**TORONTO STAR** COOKBOOK

# TORONTO STAR
# COOKBOOK

*More than 150 Diverse and Delicious Recipes*

CELEBRATING ONTARIO

# JENNIFER BAIN

*With photography by* Ryan Szulc

appetite
by RANDOM HOUSE

*Title page, clockwise from top left: Table, flaky sea, fine sea, fine sea and kosher salts*

Appetite by Random House colophon is a registered trademark

Library and Archives of Canada Cataloguing in Publication is available upon request

ISBN: 978-0-44901-569-8

Cover and text design: Terri Nimmo
Photography: Ryan Szulc
Food stylist: Noah Witenoff
Prop stylist: Madeleine Johari
Photography assistant: Matthew Gibson
Chapter illustrations: clipart.com

Printed and bound in China

Published in Canada by Appetite by Random House,
a division of Random House of Canada Limited

www.randomhouse.ca

10 9 8 7 6 5 4 3 2 1

To my hungry
husband, Rick,
my vegetarian
dancer, Lucy,
little Hazel (she
of the "squishy
tummy"), and
Charlie, who
is brand new.

# CONTENTS

# Introduction

The *Toronto Star* test kitchen has been my work home since 2000. Yes, it's unusual to have a test kitchen in the newsroom of Canada's largest newspaper, but as food editor I need to know we're publishing recipes for our readers that really work. We test all of the recipes that go into the paper. And by "we," I mostly mean "me."

I work alone in the test kitchen, which doubles as a cookbook library and my office. I do my own grocery shopping, cooking, dishes and laundry (at home, actually). I'm a journalist who cooks—not a trained chef. People think the test kitchen is big, shiny, new and full of expensive gear. In reality, when I moved in the kitchen was a forlorn place, built in 1972 and showing its age. It featured wall-to-wall carpet, unappetizing beige walls and eight malfunctioning electric burners built into an island. I had to turn one burner to high, another to medium and a third to low to cook a single dish.

When I got the opportunity to spruce things up, I first swapped the rug for black-and-red checkerboard tiles. The next year I picked hot pink paint to perk up the windowless room. Several years later I was sent to Bad Boy (former Toronto mayor Mel Lastman's discount appliance chain) for a package deal on an electric stove, fridge, dishwasher and microwave. My laminate counters are now white with colourful speckles which brighten up the retro 1970s wood cabinets. My kitchen gear is also a hodgepodge of samples sent in by companies looking for publicity and things I buy myself.

Still, I love the "Pink Palace," as I affectionately call it. When I say it's "shabby chic," most people get it. "What a nice, safe, cozy room to work in," British cooking goddess Nigella Lawson said in 2010 when she came to cook pasta from *Kitchen: Recipes From the Heart of the Home*. "A kitchen should never look decorated. It just needs to feel lived in."

## IT'S ABOUT THE RECIPES AND INGREDIENTS, NOT THE EQUIPMENT

What my test kitchen proves is this: you don't need a showroom kitchen to cook well. You need great recipes and great ingredients. I won't tell you to buy any specific pots, pans or knives (though I can't live without my electric scale and the coffee grinder I use for spices), but I will suggest that you frequent more than one supermarket, seek out grocery stores from multiple cultures and support local farmers' markets.

You'd be amazed at how many interesting ingredients have become mainstream. I used to send readers to Latin grocery stores in Toronto's Kensington Market to buy canned chipotle chilies packed in adobo sauce. Now chipotles are in most supermarkets. At one time quinoa was only available in bulk and health food stores. Now it's in Costco. I have found canned hominy, Thai curry pastes, panko bread crumbs and Sriracha hot sauce at Walmart Supercentres.

Readers wonder why we test and adapt recipes. They assume that recipes from famous chefs and celebrities work, follow them slavishly and blame themselves when they bomb. They don't realize that many talented cooks aren't always great at writing recipes. Even when the recipes work, I might adapt them by ditching a gratuitous garnish, making a smaller batch or replacing a rare ingredient with a common one, to make them more accessible to our readers at home.

I learned to cook from my mom (evolving from pint-size apple pies as a kid to deep-fried French fries as a teen). Then I went to journalism school and, when I got my first full-time reporting job, started eating out as frequently as I could. Next up, I lived in Hong Kong for two years where I cooked just a handful of times—it was cheaper and easier to eat out. When I took over the *Star*'s food beat in 2000, I wanted to write stories about the chefs, restaurants, home cooks, farmers and food people who make both Toronto and Ontario delicious. I grudgingly agreed to continue the tradition of providing *Star*-tested recipes, not yet understanding how a recipe can tell the story as much as words and photos do. I persevered, calling my mom and my Aunt Mary constantly for cooking advice, and I grew to love cooking. I don't usually create recipes from scratch, but I love to test-drive other people's creations. I take a scientific approach and use a scale, measuring tape, timer, and measuring cups and spoons to document each step. I don't take it personally when recipes fail. I either walk away, and the recipe doesn't make it into the *Star*, or I wrestle them into submission so our readers can make them with confidence.

## TORONTO IS HOME TO THE WORLD

I used to brag that my job gave me the chance to travel the world within my hometown. Toronto is one of the most multicultural cities on the planet and I've been lucky to eat my way through it for a living and tell the stories of new immigrants through their food.

Chinese chop suey restaurants and Italian pasta houses were considered exotic when I was growing up. A lot has changed. For my older daughter's first birthday party, we went to Scarborough for dim sum because kids are now hooked on Cantonese food from Hong Kong, while their parents are comfortable exploring mainland China's regional cuisines. Korean bulgogi, bibimbap and gamjatang, and Vietnamese banh mi and pho rarely need translation for food-savvy Torontonians. Japanese sushi is so ubiquitous that my older daughter made it at daycare before she even went to kindergarten.

We've slowly evolved from gorging on curries at North Indian buffets to feasting on South Indian dosas, with frequent forays into Pakistani and Sri Lankan food. My preschooler asks for mango lassis at every restaurant, Indian or not. She loves the "spongy bread" (injera) at Ethiopian restaurants, and frequently demands Tibetan beef momos.

I eat more than my share of Ethiopian food (vegetarian combos with a side of spicy lamb are my favourites). I have tracked the city's slowly evolving Mexican food scene. I can't live without Salvadoran pupusas, and have a soft spot for fiery Afghan kabobs. I've had the chance to eat Egyptian, Nigerian, Moroccan, Tunisian, Guyanese, Trinidadian, Jamaican, South African, Malaysian, Filipino, Thai, Hungarian, Greek, Lebanese, Chilean, Taiwanese, Cambodian, Colombian, Brazilian, Peruvian, Russian, Uzbek, Maltese, Turkish, Portuguese and Persian food all within Greater Toronto. I've written about Thunder Bay's Finnish pancakes, Leamington's Mexican tacos, Hamilton's unexpected diversity and Scarborough's tiny Haitian food scene. And I'm still searching for Puerto Rican, Sudanese and American soul food...

Toronto doesn't have a signature dish, though the peameal bacon sandwich is a definite frontrunner in downtown circles (don't miss Hogtown's Peameal Sandwich on page 57). Being known for one dish would be too limiting for a city of such amazing diversity. I've included recipes from more than two dozen different cultures in this book, and wish there had been space for more . . . perhaps that's for Volume Two.

## WE ARE WHAT WE EAT

The recipes in this cookbook are a curated collection of those that that have appeared in the *Toronto Star* over the years. Some come

from the era of daily recipes, some were part of the former Wednesday food section, many hail from the Chef's Showcase feature (which has run off-and-on for decades in our TV guide) and some were published as stand-alone recipes. Most came from our feature stories on food trends, cooking techniques and ingredients, or Toronto chef or restaurant profiles.

I selected recipes for the book that would tell the story of our city's exciting, evolving food scene, then our readers voted in some of their all-time favourite recipes, too (more about that on page 6). I've always tried to publish diverse recipes in the *Star* and encourage readers to explore the multitude of restaurants and grocery stores across Ontario. Remember, restaurants and stores do come and go, so call first to make sure any place mentioned here is still open. I've also included a list of my favourite shops at the end of the book where you can source some of the harder-to-find ingredients.

I tested the bulk of the recipes chosen for this book when they first appeared in the newspaper. My colleagues and freelancers tested the rest. Then, for the book, I tested every recipe again, tweaking, updating and adapting. As you start to cook the recipes at home, let me know what you think: you can email me at jbain@thestar.ca, or find me on Facebook (facebook/thesaucylady) and Twitter (@thesaucylady).

### CAN I FREEZE THAT?

As a food editor, people ask me for advice about cooking all the time. To help you get started, here are the answers to the five questions I am asked most regularly:

# Question 1: "Why are you always on about kosher salt?"

Kosher salt (used to make meat kosher) is additive free and has larger crystals than table salt so it's easier to control. It's the darling of chefs and foodies, and available in every supermarket now. Sea salt, which is harvested from evaporated seawater instead of salt mines, is another good choice. It can be fine or flaky, and I adore the flaky version as a finishing salt.

I rarely use table salt because it is refined and contains additives like iodine and anti-caking agents. The fine granules are very salty and it's easy to use too much when you're seasoning a dish, although I occasionally use it when I'm baking because it melts evenly into cake and cookie batters.

# Question 2: "Why are your portions so small?"

Most of us eat too much and have a skewed sense of proper portions so I've tried to reign in serving sizes. You can download a free copy of *Eating Well with Canada's Food Guide* from Health Canada at hc-sc.gc.ca and see how small a portion should be. For example, a recommended serving of meat or meat alternatives weighs 2-½ ounces (75 g). Adults should have two to three servings per day, spread out over breakfast, lunch and dinner—which means having an 8-ounce (225 g) steak for dinner more than uses up your full daily meat intake.

## Question 4: "Can I freeze this?"

Probably. I tend to eat my food immediately or as leftovers because, when I freeze things, they get forgotten. But, if you have the knack for wrapping and freezing food, please go ahead.

## Question 5: "What should I eat this with?"

Honestly, whatever you like. I believe in well-balanced eating more than well-balanced meals. I might eat leftover Thai vegetable curry and rice for breakfast, a spicy pork gyro for lunch and a big salad and tons of fruit for dinner. If, at the end of the day, you've eaten mostly vegetables, fruits and grains with some dairy and meat or meat alternatives, you've done just fine.

### THE SAUCY LADY EATS AGAIN

My Saucy Lady column covers all of my eating and drinking adventures. I don't just cook, I research and write about chefs, home cooks, cookbooks, restaurants, celebrities, farmers, artisans, food trends and food events. I borrowed the column's name from a 1977 cookbook that I found in a used bookstore: *Saucy Ladies: 150 Delicate Sauces Accompanied by 60 Indelicate Ladies*, by Ron Stieglitz and Sandy Lesberg. Ron and Sandy set out to "liberate" people from outdated theories on sauce making and show how easy it is to make elegant sauces. "Sauces are for all who try," they write, "and we encourage you to be adventurous."

Cooking is for all who try, too. Please be adventurous.

## Question 3: "I don't like/ am allergic to (fill in the blank), so can I cut that out of the recipe?"

I can only vouch for the recipes as tested, but I wholeheartedly urge you to experiment and adapt.

## *Star* READERS SPEAK OUT

I asked *Toronto Star* readers to nominate their favourite recipes for this cookbook and the emails and letters came pouring in. It was hard to narrow down the selection but, in the end, I chose recipes that best reflect how the city and province cook and eat now. You'll find the "Readers' Choice" nominees throughout the book. Sadly there wasn't room for all our readers' favourites and many popular recipes didn't make it in. I'd like to share a few of the rave reviews I received about dishes that couldn't be included, to illustrate what great recipes can mean to people. (Drop me an email if you'd like any of these recipes.)

"One of my most treasured possessions is my late mother's recipe box," writes June Hagerman of Stirling, Ont., nominating a *Star* **Sour Cream Coffee Cake** and a **Laura Secord Old-Fashioned Lemon Bread.** "The box includes handwritten recipes on index cards and scraps of paper and recipe clippings from the *Toronto Star*, and is a most meaningful legacy. I am my mother's child. I, too, have my personal recipe binder with my notes and clippings, something that I hope the next generation will appreciate."

_____

"As long-time subscribers of the *Toronto Star*, we have cut out our share of recipes," writes Paula Osmok of Lindsay, Ont., rooting for **Scottish Shortbread**. "They now take their place alongside treasured family recipes for comfort foods that, when served, elicit great childhood memories and lively conversations."

_____

"I have lots of recipes from the *Star*," writes Julie Lang of Toronto, nominating **Meatloaf-in-the-Round** originally from *Chatelaine*. "I used to clip all the time. Now I have so many recipes I have to control myself and be more picky. I've given Meatloaf-in the-Round to dozens of people. It really is popular in our household."

———

"I have this recipe memorized and make it at least once a week," writes Dale Marcotte of Barrie, Ont., about **Blackberry and Raspberry Dutch Baby**, adapted from *Food & Wine*. "I have cut down the butter to one tablespoon and, as you noted, different berries can be used. I tried a regular pan, just to see if it would work because my two daughters didn't own cast iron skillets. I then went out and bought them their own skillets after discovering that you must use a cast iron one."

———

"Here is the best recipe I have clipped from the *Star*," writes Jane Allison of Hillier, Ont., referring to a **Maple-Pecan Pie** adapted from *Bon Appétit*. "Yes, my copy is stained and discoloured but that just means it's been used lots! Every time I make this pie it gets rave reviews and, yes, it is hard to part with my clipping, but to have it end up in your cookbook for others to enjoy would be great."

———

Tim Garrett emailed from Manitoba to nominate **Smoked Paprika Chicken Thighs with Lentil Stew**, a recipe from American chef José Andrés from *Food & Wine*. "I had never used smoked paprika, so thought 'no time like the present.' This dish rocked! Everything worked in harmony and it gave meaning to the phrase 'comfort food.' I live in Winnipeg and was having this for dinner as I watched snow blowing around outside . . . but it was warm inside!"

———

Dave Ackerman of Toronto emailed to compliment a **Punjabi Rajma** recipe that I featured from Indian celebrity chef Sanjeev Kapoor. "My son and his wife are vegetarians so we have it quite often when they come to visit. Everyone who tries it really likes it."

———

"Rocked my socks off and then some," writes Daniel Monette about a **Homemade Paneer** recipe from Vancouver author Bal Arneson.

———

"Never has a recipe created as much of a 'stir' in our family as this one," emails Gloria Martin of Toronto about a recipe from 1999 called **Million-Dollar Chicken**. "I made it, loved it and passed it on to family and friends. It's delicious and everyone puts their own special twist on it. Million-Dollar Chicken has spread through our family as far north as Sault Ste. Marie, Ontario, and as far south as Toledo, Ohio."

———

"I made a lifestyle change in my eating habits last July," writes Frances M. Currie of Brantford, Ont. "One of the things I introduced to my diet was quinoa, and the **Cumin Quinoa with Beets** is a favourite way of using it. P.S. The **Sumac Yogurt** side dish puts it over the top. Yum."

———

"I used to be a single mom and for many years my younger brother and his wife welcomed me and the kids to their cottage near Kapuskasing, Ontario, for a week each summer," writes Patricia Murray of Toronto,

nominating **Grilled Sirloin with Chili Rub and Horseradish Sauce** from Weber (the barbecue makers). "I would always prepare dinner for our hosts when they arrived Friday night. I was trying to do the best on the cheap, so this recipe was a big hit and remains a favourite."

———

"I *love* the recipe for **Soba with Spicy Peanut Sauce**," writes Jessica Ludgate of Quebec City. "It has everything: sweet, spicy and, best of all, peanut butter. It makes six servings but I made an entire recipe for two of us and we ate half of it. The next day I took the remainder for my lunch and had a recipe request from four co-workers, none of whom speak much English but all were more than willing to stumble their way through the recipe to make such a wonderful dish."

———

"In your 2011 Cookie Calendar, I was pleased to note that the first cookie you presented, **Peppermint Crisps**, was dairy- and egg-free," writes Susan Hawrylow of Whitby, Ont. "Also offered was a gluten-free cookie,

**Spiced Chocolate Crackles**. Nowadays, when there are so many people with food allergies, intolerances and health issues, it is great to be able to find a variety of recipes to suit each of our unique needs."

———

"Raised in a traditional British household, shortbread cookies were always a part of Christmas baking," writes Janet Vanier of Mississauga, Ont., praising **Curry Coriander Shorties**. "However, when I married a man from Guyana, I quickly found out that my cooking was very bland in the eyes— and taste buds—of my in-laws. Imagine my delight in finding a recipe that combined my favourite Christmas cookie with the curry flavour that my husband's family so enjoys."

———

"From being a child of 11 who wanted to learn about cooking easy and delicious foods, through my phase as a vegetarian, hippy, food-conscious commune-dweller, to the independent woman I am now, who loves to eat and prepare easy, nutritious food, the *Star* has been there for me," writes Honey Novick of Toronto, with her letter's envelope stuffed full of clippings. "I learned to cook, in part, from reading and clipping recipes in the *Star*. It's almost like an interactive way of appreciating the newspaper."

———

"I now have four thick folders filled with recipes that I have collected over the years, along with a huge library of cookbooks (about 132) covering a very diverse range of tastes. I like to read cookbooks as others read novels," writes Janice Bernstein of Toronto, nominating four favourite *Star* recipes. "Over the years, I have found cooking to be very therapeutic. There is nothing quite like slicing, chopping, beating or stirring to take one's mind off problems. And the feeling of achievement when you taste the fruits of your labour does wonders for your self-esteem."

———

"Years ago my husband clipped a recipe from the *Star* and asked me to try it. Now, I'm not much of a baker, but decided to have a go," writes Kris Stinnissen of Wawa, Ont., nominating **Old-Fashioned Scones** from 2002. "Alas, I lost the treasured recipe and have done countless online searches for it. Today I was tidying up my cookbook shelf, and guess what fell out? The recipe! So I must share. They are the best scones I ever ate, and a piece of cake to make."

———

"My husband says this is the best macaroni and cheese he ever tasted,"

writes Wanda Allan of Etobicoke, Ont, nominating **Pimiento Mac 'n' Cheese**. "One of my grandsons went home and told his mom how good it is. It's the pimientos that make it."

———

"The **Best-Ever Banana Muffins** never fail to impress and have won me great reviews over the years," writes Jacki Nelson of Toronto. "The recipe is so simple and they taste superb."

———

"I am including this clipping that has made it into the Niederbuhl Family Cookbook as a forever favourite," writes Casey Miller of Markham, Ont., nominating **Fruit and Nut Biscotti**. "The recipe has been photocopied, scanned and sent to friends and relatives as far away as Australia. The biscotti are good any time, as a treat or a healthy snack, but are a must-have on our sweets tray at holiday time."

———

# BREAKFAST AND BRUNCH

My favourite meal,
no matter what
time of day I eat it.

*Left: Brown sugar, steel-cut oats, large flake oats*

## » MANGO LASSI

MAKES 2 SERVINGS

1 cup (250 mL) plain yogurt
½ cup (125 mL) canned
    mango pulp
5 ice cubes
1 tbsp (15 mL) granulated sugar
Water as needed

Mango lassi, a staple in Indian restaurants, is a favourite with my kids. The trick to making this delicious drink rich, creamy and consistent is canned mango pulp. Look for it in Indian and Asian supermarkets (any brand will do). This is how we like our lassi, but feel free to tinker.

**1.** In a blender, combine the yogurt, mango pulp, ice and sugar. Blend on high speed until smooth, about 2 minutes. If the mixture is too thick, add a little water and blend again. Pour into 2 glasses.

## FRESH'S POMEGRANATE-BLUEBERRY SMOOTHIE

MAKES 1 LARGE OR
2 SMALL SERVINGS

1 cup (250 mL) bottled
    pomegranate juice (such as
    POM Wonderful)
1 fresh or frozen banana, peeled
    and broken into several pieces
3 ice cubes
2 tbsp (30 mL) fresh or frozen
    blueberries

The recipe for this gorgeous garnet drink comes from Ruth Tal's Fresh (freshrestaurants.ca) vegetarian restaurant. I first tried it at the 2007 Toronto Taste (torontotaste.ca), an annual gourmet graze for Canada's largest food rescue program, Second Harvest (secondharvest.ca). The non-profit picks up donated excess fresh food daily from supermarkets, manufacturers, restaurants and caterers and delivers it to social service programs.

**1.** In a blender, combine the pomegranate juice and banana. Blend on low speed for 1 minute. Add the ice and blueberries, then blend on high speed until smooth, about 1 minute. Pour into 1 or 2 glasses.

This is a "power shake" at Fresh (freshrestaurants.ca) and it satisfies like a snack or small meal. Some dried dates need to be soaked but, if you use plump, succulent Medjool dates, you can skip the soaking step.

The recipe also appears in the restaurant's fourth cookbook, *Fresh: New Vegetarian and Vegan Recipes from the Award-winning Fresh Restaurants* (John Wiley & Sons, 2011) by Ruth Tal and Jennifer Houston.

## FRESH'S DATE-ALMOND SHAKE

≪

MAKES 1 LARGE OR
2 SMALL SERVINGS

4 dried honey or Medjool dates, pitted
1 cup (250 mL) regular or vanilla soy milk
1 fresh or frozen banana, peeled and broken into pieces
3 ice cubes
1 tbsp (15 mL) crunchy or smooth almond butter
1 tsp (5 mL) pure maple syrup
Pinch ground cinnamon

**1.** If using honey dates, soak them in a small bowl of hot water for 5 minutes, then drain well.

**2.** In a blender, combine the dates, soy milk and banana, and blend on low speed for 1 minute.

**3.** Add the ice, almond butter, maple syrup and cinnamon, and blend on high speed until smooth, about 2 minutes. Pour into 1 or 2 glasses.

"This recipe has been served to people from all over the world. I make it to take to events, feed guests or any time or place I need to take food. They are the most moist muffin and everyone loves them."

**JOANN KROPF-HEDLEY,** COBOURG, ONT.

Mercury Espresso Bar (mercuryespresso.com) used to sell a millet version of these clever muffins. I was bereft when they disappeared until I found a recipe in *Rebar: Modern Food Cookbook* (Big Ideas, 2001) by Victoria restaurateurs Audrey Alsterberg and Wanda Urbanowicz, and began tinkering at home.

**1.** Preheat the oven to 350°F (180°C) Grease a 12-cup muffin pan.

**2.** In a small, dry skillet over medium heat, toast the quinoa until lightly browned, fragrant and just starting to pop, about 4 minutes.

**3.** Transfer the quinoa to a large bowl. Add the pumpkin, buttermilk, sugar, oil, eggs, 3 tbsp (45 mL) pumpkin seeds and the vanilla, and mix well. Stir in the oats.

**4.** In a medium bowl, whisk together the all-purpose and whole wheat flours, baking powder, baking soda, salt, cinnamon, ginger and nutmeg. Add the flour mixture to the pumpkin mixture and stir gently just until the dry ingredients are moistened.

**5.** Spoon the batter evenly into the prepared muffin pan (the cups will be very full and the cooked muffins will have large tops). Sprinkle the tops with the remaining 1 tbsp (15 mL) pumpkin seeds.

**6.** Bake in the centre of the oven until a cake tester inserted in the centre of a muffin comes out mostly clean and the tops are browned, 20 to 25 minutes.

**7.** Let the muffins cool in the pan for 10 minutes, then remove them from the pan and let cool on a wire rack. Serve warm or at room temperature. Store the muffins in an airtight container for up to 2 days.

# PUMPKIN-QUINOA MUFFINS

**READERS' CHOICE**

MAKES 12

½ cup (125 mL) dried quinoa, unrinsed

1-½ cups (375 mL) canned pure pumpkin

1 cup (250 mL) well-shaken buttermilk

¾ cup (185 mL) packed light brown sugar

½ cup (125 mL) canola oil

2 large eggs, beaten

¼ cup (60 mL) raw, green, shelled pumpkin seeds (pepitas)

1 tsp (5 mL) pure vanilla extract

½ cup (125 mL) large-flake oats

1 cup (250 mL) all-purpose flour

¾ cup (185 mL) whole wheat flour

2 tsp (10 mL) baking powder

1-½ tsp (7 mL) baking soda

½ tsp (2 mL) kosher salt

½ tsp (2 mL) ground cinnamon

½ tsp (2 mL) ground ginger

¼ tsp (1 mL) freshly grated nutmeg

## » MITZI'S OATMEAL PANCAKES WITH BERRY COMPOTE AND MAPLE BUTTER

MAKES ABOUT 10

**Berry Compote**
3 cups (750 mL) raspberries or
    blueberries
½ cup (125 mL) granulated sugar
½ cup (125 mL) water

**Maple Butter**
½ cup (125 mL) unsalted butter,
    at room temperature
2 tbsp (30 mL) pure maple syrup

**Oatmeal Pancakes**
3 cups (750 mL) quick oats (not
    instant or large-flake)
3 cups (750 mL) well-shaken
    buttermilk
½ cup (125 mL) all-purpose
    flour
2 tbsp (30 mL) packed light
    brown sugar
1 tsp (5 mL) baking soda
1 tsp (5 mL) baking powder
2 large eggs
⅓ cup (80 mL) unsalted butter,
    melted and cooled
Oil for cooking

Feast of Fields (feastoffields.org), organized by Organic Advocates, is a roving picnic feast/fundraiser held annually to support organic projects. I scored this recipe at the 2001 event when Mitzi's Café (mitzis.ca) served up these substantial pancakes. I love how they're thick with oats and tangy from buttermilk, and like to serve them topped with maple butter and berry compote, but you can just drizzle them with warm maple syrup if you prefer. Mitzi's Café still serves variations of these pancakes.

**1.** For the Berry Compote, simmer the berries, sugar and water in a medium saucepan over medium heat, stirring often, until the berries break down and form a sauce, about 30 minutes.

**2.** For the Maple Butter, in a small bowl, mash together the butter and maple syrup with a fork until smooth.

**3.** For the Oatmeal Pancakes, in a large bowl, soak the oats in 2-½ cups (625 mL) buttermilk for 15 minutes.

**4.** In a small bowl, whisk together the flour, sugar, baking soda and baking powder. In a second small bowl, whisk together the eggs and butter. Add first the flour mixture, then the egg mixture to the oats, along with the remaining ½ cup (125 mL) buttermilk. Mix well with a wooden spoon. The batter will be thick.

**5.** Heat a large non-stick skillet over medium-high heat, then brush with oil. Using ½ cup (125 mL) batter per pancake, cook the pancakes in batches until golden and cooked through, about 5 minutes per side.

**6.** Serve the pancakes with the Berry Compote and Maple Butter.

Ontario sweet potatoes are nutritional all-stars that aren't potatoes at all, but are part of the morning glory family. They're grown by farmers such as Bob Proracki, who operates Round Plains Plantation (ontariosweetpotato.com) in what used to be tobacco territory.

Bob's wife, Juli, who turns out muffins, tarts, spreads and dips from their registered kitchen and sells them at Toronto farmers' markets, shared this recipe with me during a 2006 visit to their Waterford farm. These are nourishing, not flashy, muffins but they're lovely and moist with a hint of spice.

## ONTARIO SWEET POTATO AND APPLE MUFFINS «

MAKES 12

¾ cup (185 mL) oat bran
¾ cup (185 mL) whole wheat flour
⅔ cup (160 mL) packed light brown sugar
1 tsp (5 mL) baking powder
1 tsp (5 mL) baking soda
1-½ tsp (7 mL) ground cinnamon
Pinch table salt
1 cup (250 mL) peeled, cooked and mashed sweet potato
½ cup (125 mL) peeled, cored and finely diced apples
⅔ cup (160 mL) plain yogurt
2 large eggs
3 tbsp (45 mL) canola oil

1. Preheat the oven to 350°F (180°C). Grease a 12-cup muffin pan.

2. In a large mixing bowl, stir together the oat bran, flour, sugar, baking powder, baking soda, cinnamon and salt. Stir in the sweet potato, apples, yogurt, eggs and oil just until the dry ingredients are moistened.

3. Spoon the batter evenly into the prepared muffin pan. Bake in the centre of the oven until the tops are firm and a cake tester inserted in the centre of a muffin comes out clean, 20 to 25 minutes.

4. Let the muffins cool in the pan for 10 minutes, then remove from the pan and let them cool on a wire rack. Serve warm or at room temperature. Store the muffins in an airtight container for up to 2 days.

## » JOSHNA MAHARAJ'S BUTTERMILK SCONES

MAKES ABOUT 12

3 cups (750 mL) all-purpose flour
⅓ cup (80 mL) granulated sugar
¾ tsp (4 mL) baking powder
½ tsp (2 mL) baking soda
½ tsp (2 mL) kosher salt
¾ cup (185 mL) unsalted butter, frozen
1 cup (250 mL) chopped fruit or nuts, or grated cheese (optional)
2 tbsp (30 mL) chopped fresh herbs (optional)
1 tbsp (15 mL) finely grated lemon and/or lime zest (optional)
1-⅓ cups (330 mL) well-shaken buttermilk
1 tbsp (15 mL) additional buttermilk or milk or cream for brushing tops
Coarse brown turbinado sugar or flaky sea salt for dusting

The secret of these flaky scones is frozen butter. Keep your hot hands away from the butter and handle the dough as little as possible. This versatile recipe comes from Toronto chef and food activist Joshna Maharaj (joshnamaharaj.posterous.com), who has worked for the Stop Community Food Centre and helped revamp patient menus at Scarborough Hospital. My favourite combo is blueberries and lemon zest.

**1.** Preheat the oven to 425°F (220°C). Line 2 baking sheets with parchment paper.

**2.** In a large mixing bowl, stir or whisk together the flour, sugar, baking powder, baking soda and salt.

**3.** Using a food processor fitted with a large grater attachment, quickly grate the butter. Or use the large holes of a box grater. Add the butter to the flour mixture. Using your fingertips, toss the flour mixture over the butter to gently combine. If using any fruits, nuts, cheese, herbs or zest, add them now, tossing gently to combine with the flour mixture.

**4.** Make a well in the centre of the mixture and add 1-⅓ cups (330 mL) buttermilk. Using a fork, stir the mixture until it just comes together and a soft dough forms. Turn the dough out onto a large sheet of parchment paper and gently press to form a 12- x 8-inch (30 x 20 cm) rectangle that's about 1 inch (2.5 cm) thick.

**5.** Using the parchment paper, fold the dough in half, pressing gently. (The paper keeps your body heat from melting the butter.) Continue to fold and press the dough, incorporating any dry bits that fall out, until the dough just comes together.

**6.** Press the dough gently through the paper to again form a 12- x 8-inch (30 x 20 cm) rectangle that's about 1 inch (2.5 cm) thick. Cut the dough into 12 triangles or any other shapes you like. Arrange the scones, 1 inch (2.5 cm) apart, on the prepared baking sheets.

**7.** Using a pastry brush, brush the tops of the scones with 1 tbsp (15 mL) buttermilk, milk or cream, then sprinkle them generously with turbinado sugar or flaky sea salt, depending on what flavourings you've added.

**8.** Bake until firm to the touch and lightly golden, about 10 to 14 minutes. Transfer the scones to a wire rack to cool. Serve warm or at room temperature. Store in an airtight container for up to 1 day.

Pastry chef Rachelle Cadwell owns Beast restaurant (thebeast-restaurant.com) with her husband, Scott Vivian. She handles the pastry and front-of-house duties, while he does the rest of the cooking. These fluffy buttermilk biscuits appear at Sunday brunch, on their own or turned into a "Beastwich" sandwich, with different fillings each week.

# BEAST'S BUTTERMILK BISCUITS

### MAKES ABOUT 12

2 cups (500 mL) all-purpose
    flour, plus more for sprinkling
2-½ tsp (12 mL) baking powder
1 tsp (5 mL) baking soda
1-½ tsp (7 mL) granulated sugar
¾ tsp (4 mL) fine sea salt
¼ tsp (1 mL) freshly ground
    black pepper
¼ cup (60 mL) cold unsalted
    butter
¾ cup (185 mL) well-shaken
    buttermilk
¼ cup (60 mL) whipping cream,
    plus more for brushing

**1.** Preheat the oven to 400°F (200°C) oven. Line a large baking sheet with parchment paper.

**2.** In a large bowl and using a fine-mesh sieve, sift together 2 cups (500 mL) flour, the baking powder and baking soda. Stir in the sugar, salt and pepper.

**3.** Using the large holes of a box grater, quickly grate the cold butter into the flour mixture. Mix with your fingertips until the mixture resembles coarse meal.

**4.** Slowly add the buttermilk and ¼ cup (60 mL) cream, gently working the mixture with your hands until a dough forms. Do not overwork the dough or the biscuits will be tough.

**5.** Turn the dough onto a lightly floured surface. Sprinkle with flour, if needed, then gently roll out to ¾-inch (2 cm) thickness. Use a 2-½-inch (6 cm) round cookie cutter to punch out the biscuits. Press the scraps of dough together and repeat until all the dough is used.

**6.** Put the biscuits on the prepared baking sheet and brush the tops with cream.

**7.** Bake on the upper rack of the oven until the tops are lightly golden, 13 to 15 minutes. Transfer the biscuits to a wire rack to cool. Serve warm or at room temperature. Store in an airtight container for up to 1 day.

## » PITA BREAK'S POACHED EGGS IN SPICY TOMATO STEW

### (SHAKSHUKA)

MAKES 4 SERVINGS

2 tbsp (30 mL) extra virgin olive oil
1 medium yellow onion, chopped
2 green onions, sliced
4 cloves garlic, minced
1-½ cups (375 mL) water
2 plum (roma) tomatoes, chopped
1 green bell pepper, seeded and chopped
1 red bell pepper, seeded and chopped
1 can (5-½ oz/156 mL) tomato paste
6 cremini mushrooms, thinly sliced
2 tbsp (30 mL) ketchup
1 tbsp (15 mL) fresh lemon juice
2 tsp (10 mL) dried oregano
1 tsp (5 mL) dried red chili flakes, or to taste
4 large eggs
Pita bread (preferably whole wheat or multigrain) for serving

Ozery's Pita Break in North York (pitabreak.com) is known for its thick, fresh, chewy pita breads. When I toured the bakery in 2004, co-founder Alon Ozery explained how his family make pitas using their grandmother's recipe, wholesome ingredients and no preservatives. The Ozerys, who have ties to Yemen and Israel, shared this brunch favourite which they serve with everything from pitas, bagels, cheeses, olives, pickles, hummus and salads to cream cheese and lox. If you don't like mushrooms or bell peppers, Alon suggests adding chopped spinach.

**1.** In a medium non-stick saucepan or skillet, heat the oil over medium-high heat. Add the yellow and green onions and garlic, then cook, stirring, for 7 minutes.

**2.** Stir in the water, tomatoes, green and red peppers, tomato paste, mushrooms, ketchup, lemon juice, oregano and red chili flakes. Increase the heat to high and bring to a boil. Reduce the heat to low, then simmer, covered for 30 minutes, stirring occasionally.

**3.** Crack 1 egg into a small bowl, being careful not to break the yolk. Gently slide the egg directly onto the vegetable mixture. Repeat with the remaining eggs, leaving a space between each one.

**4.** Increase the heat to medium-low and cover the saucepan. Cook until the egg whites have mostly solidified but the yolks are still soft and runny, 5 to 7 minutes. (Cook a little longer if you prefer firmer yolks.)

**5.** To serve, carefully ladle out among 4 bowls, including 1 egg with each portion. Serve with pita bread.

## » FRANKLY EATERY'S EGGS BHURJI

MAKES 2 SERVINGS

4 large eggs
2 tbsp (30 mL) cream
    (preferably half-and-half)
Kosher salt to taste
1 to 2 tbsp (15 to 30 mL)
    vegetable oil
¼ cup (60 mL) finely diced
    yellow onion
¼ cup (60 mL) diced tomatoes
2 tbsp (30 mL) frozen peas,
    thawed
2 tsp (10 mL) minced, peeled
    ginger
¼ tsp (1 mL) turmeric
Large pinch cayenne

These Indian-spiced eggs come from Frankly Eatery, a popular Leslieville restaurant, run by brother-and-sister duo Alka Graham and Rick Chander, that's now closed. "The key to making a great egg bhurji is to make sure there is enough salt to complement the amount of cayenne you've added," says Alka, who created the recipe with her mom, Kaushalya Chander. In India, eggs bhurji is often served with rotis or bread, but Alka likes it with simple mixed greens and baguette.

**1.** In a large bowl, whisk together the eggs, cream and salt until thoroughly combined.

**2.** In a medium non-stick skillet, heat 1 tbsp (15 mL) oil over medium heat. Add the onion, then cook, stirring, until it's translucent, about 3 minutes. Add the tomatoes, then cook, stirring, until they begin to dissolve, about 2 minutes.

**3.** Add the peas and ginger, reduce heat to low and cook, stirring, for 1 minute. Add the turmeric and cayenne and cook, stirring, for 30 seconds. If the skillet looks dry, add the remaining 1 tbsp (15 mL) oil.

**4.** Increase the heat to medium and add the egg mixture. Cook, without stirring, until the eggs start to set at the edges, then gently stir with a wooden spoon until the eggs are cooked through, but not brown, and large curds form, 1-½ to 2 minutes. Serve immediately.

During my stint as a brunch columnist, I ate restaurant eggs in every guise imaginable. Here are three simple ways I jazz up ordinary eggs. Always crack your egg into a bowl and slide it into the skillet without breaking the yolk or including any shell fragments. If you opt for the Chocolate-Chili version, remember that Asian chili oil is powerful stuff so don't use too much.

# FRIED EGGS THREE WAYS

MAKES 1 SERVING OF
WHICHEVER EGG YOU CHOOSE

**Balsamic Fried Egg**
1 tbsp (15 mL) fruity extra virgin
    olive oil
1 large egg
1 slice buttered toast
1 tbsp (15 mL) aged balsamic
    vinegar

**Maple Fried Egg**
1 tbsp (15 mL) unsalted butter
1 large egg
1 slice buttered toast
1 tbsp (15 mL) pure maple syrup

**Chocolate-Chili Fried Egg**
1 tsp (5 mL) Asian chili oil
1 large egg
1 slice buttered toast
1 tsp (5 mL) finely grated dark
    chocolate (at least 70% cocoa
    solids)

**1.** For the Balsamic Fried Egg, heat a medium skillet over medium heat. Add the oil, then the egg and cook for 30 seconds. Using a silicone basting brush, baste the top of the egg with oil to help it cook. Cook to desired doneness (60 to 90 seconds for a runny yolk). Using a spatula, slide the egg onto the toast set on a plate. Discard the oil from the skillet. Add the vinegar to the skillet and let sizzle and reduce for 15 to 30 seconds before drizzling it over the egg.

**2.** For the Maple Fried Egg, heat a medium skillet over medium heat. Add the butter, then the egg and cook for 30 seconds. Using a silicone basting brush, baste the top of the egg with butter to help it cook. Cook to desired doneness (60 to 90 seconds for a runny yolk). Using a spatula, slide the egg onto the toast set on a plate. Add the maple syrup to the skillet and let sizzle and reduce for 15 to 30 seconds before drizzling it over the egg.

**3.** For the Chocolate-Chili Fried Egg, heat a medium skillet over medium heat. Add the oil, then the egg and cook for 30 seconds. Using a silicone basting brush, baste the top of the egg with oil to help it cook. Cook to desired doneness (60 to 90 seconds for a runny yolk). Using a spatula, slide the egg onto the toast set on a plate and sprinkle the egg with the chocolate.

## » MEXICAN CHORIZO AND SCRAMBLED EGG TACOS

### READERS' CHOICE

MAKES ABOUT 12 (SERVING 4-6)

**Tacos**

1 tbsp (15 mL) vegetable oil

8 oz (225 g) fresh Mexican chorizo or other chili-spiced pork sausage, casings discarded

½ medium white onion, finely chopped

1 jalapeño pepper, stemmed and minced (seeded if desired)

2 large cloves garlic, minced

3 plum (roma) tomatoes, finely diced

4 large eggs, beaten

Chopped leaves from ½ bunch cilantro

12 small corn tortillas (about 6 inches/15 cm)

**Toppings (optional)**

1 ripe avocado, sliced or chopped

Grated mild cheese, such as mozzarella or Mexican queso fresco

Salsa verde or red Mexican salsa

Lime wedges for serving

"This is very 'tweakable,' which is important for our health and digestive systems, and it also contains ingredients that are readily available in our home. It's easy to throw together and doesn't tie me up in the kitchen all day."

**JACKIE ROBINSON,** BRAMPTON, ONT.

I've been tracking Toronto's slowly emerging Mexican food scene since 2000. You'll often find me in Kensington Market buying Mexican chorizo from Segovia Meats, fresh tortillas from La Tortilleria or packaged tortillas from Perola's, a Latin grocery store. I like Herdez salsas.

As part of the *Toronto Star* Speakers Bureau, I once taught a high school cooking club how to make these tacos since they symbolize my eating philosophy: They're bursting with flavour, demand personalization and are relatively easy to make.

**1.** For the tacos, heat the oil in a large non-stick skillet over medium heat. Add the sausage and cook, breaking up the meat into small pieces with a wooden spoon, until the sausage is cooked through, 8 to 10 minutes. With a slotted spoon, transfer the sausage to a bowl.

**2.** Return the skillet with the sausage drippings to medium heat. Add the onion, jalapeño and garlic, and cook, stirring, for 5 minutes. Add the tomatoes, with their juices. Increase the heat to medium-high and cook, stirring often, until the liquid evaporates, about 5 minutes.

**3.** Return the sausage to the skillet. Add the eggs and cook, stirring slowly, until they are tender and creamy. Stir in the cilantro and transfer to a bowl.

**4.** Heat each tortilla in small, dry skillet over medium-high heat for about 15 seconds per side. Alternatively, microwave each tortilla for about 10 seconds. Wrap the tortillas in a clean tea towel to keep them warm, and put them on a plate.

**5.** If using toppings, put the avocado, cheese and salsa in 3 separate serving bowls.

**6.** To assemble, spoon a heaping ¼ cup (60 mL) of sausage-and-egg mixture onto the centre of each tortilla. Sprinkle with avocado, cheese and salsa (if using). Fold the tortillas in half to eat. Serve with lime wedges.

## » CRÊPES WITH SMOKED SALMON, RED ONIONS AND GOAT CHEESE

MAKES ABOUT 6

**Batter**

3 large eggs
1-¼ cups (310 mL) milk
⅔ cup (160 mL) all-purpose
   flour
⅓ cup (80 mL) barley flour
1 tbsp (15 mL) granulated sugar
½ tsp (2 mL) kosher salt
¼ cup (60 mL) vegetable oil,
   plus more for cooking

**Filling**

1-½ cups (375 mL) crumbled
   chèvre (soft unripened goat
   cheese)
6 thin slices smoked salmon, or
   to taste
½ cup (125 mL) very thinly
   sliced red onion
6 tbsp (90 mL) pure maple
   syrup

Véronique Perez has brought much joy to Torontonians with Crêpes à GoGo (crepesagogo.com). Her signature crêpe is filled with raspberry jam and mozzarella, but she creates all kinds of sweet and savoury versions. My daughter Lucy loves crêpes sprinkled with sugar and drizzled with fresh lemon juice, while I'm partial to either Nutella and sliced bananas or this sweet-savoury smoked salmon and goat cheese combo.

**1.** For the batter, whisk together the eggs and milk in a medium bowl. Set aside.

**2.** Sift the all-purpose and barley flours through a fine-mesh sieve into a large bowl. Stir in the sugar and salt.

**3.** Slowly whisk the egg mixture into the flour mixture until well combined. Whisk in ¼ cup (60 mL) oil. If the batter is lumpy, pass it through the sieve. Cover and let stand at room temperature for 2 hours.

**4.** When ready to cook, heat a large non-stick skillet over medium-high heat, then brush with oil. Ladle ⅓ cup (80 mL) batter into the centre of the skillet. Remove the skillet from the heat and quickly tilt it, swirling the batter to form a thin crêpe that's about 7 inches (18 cm) in diameter.

**5.** Cook until the top is no longer wet and the edges are papery, about 1 minute. Carefully flip the crêpe, then cook until the underside is lightly browned, about 30 seconds. Transfer the crêpe to a large plate, then repeat with the remaining batter, stacking each crêpe on the plate as it cooks.

**6.** For the filling, lay 6 crêpes in a single layer on a work surface. (Wrap and refrigerate any remaining crêpes for another use.) Working left to right, sprinkle cheese to form a 2-inch (5-cm) band in the centre of each crêpe. Top each with 1 or 2 pieces of smoked salmon and equal portions of onion. Drizzle each portion of smoked salmon with 1 tbsp (15 mL) maple syrup.

**7.** Fold the bottom of each crêpe up over the filling, bringing it to 1 inch (2.5 cm) short of the top. Working from the bottom, roll up each crêpe, then cut in half crosswise. Serve at room temperature.

Congee is a Chinese rice gruel that serves as a neutral backdrop to infinite toppings. I used to love the cross-cultural sweet and savoury versions (a Mexican-influenced congee with tomatillo salsa, pumpkin seeds, roasted garlic and soy was a favourite) that chef Brock Shepherd created at his restaurant Azul. Brock now owns Burger Bar (theburgerbar.ca) in Kensington Market and doesn't serve congee, but he pulled out an old recipe for me.

I like this with chicken but feel free to get creative with your toppings. For a sweet version, try honey or maple syrup, vanilla extract, lime juice, garam masala or Chinese five-spice powder, plus berries, or diced apples or pears. If you want to save time, make congee from leftover cooked rice.

# BROCK SHEPHERD'S CONGEE WITH EGG

≪

MAKES 4 SERVINGS

**Congee**
9 cups (2.25 L) water
1 cup (250 mL) long-grain white
   or brown rice
Kosher salt to taste

**Toppings**
1 tbsp (15 mL) extra virgin olive
   oil
6 cloves garlic, minced
Shredded, cooked chicken to
   taste (optional)
2 green onions, very thinly
   sliced
1 tbsp (15 mL) minced, peeled
   ginger
Soy sauce for serving
Sesame oil for serving
2 large eggs, beaten

**1.** For the congee, in a large, heavy-bottomed pot, bring the water and rice to a boil over high heat. Partially cover with a lid, then reduce the heat to medium or medium-low (just enough to maintain a simmer).

**2.** Simmer, stirring occasionally to prevent sticking and reducing the heat if necessary, until the rice breaks down and becomes thick and porridge-like, 60 to 90 minutes for white rice or 2 to 3 hours for brown rice. Season with salt to taste.

**3.** For the toppings, heat the oil in a small skillet over medium-high. Add the garlic, then cook, stirring, until browned, 5 to 7 minutes. Transfer to a small serving bowl.

**4.** Put the chicken (if using), green onions, ginger, soy sauce and sesame oil in separate small serving bowls.

**5.** Slowly drizzle the eggs into the hot congee, whisking or stirring constantly, so the eggs blend into the congee without scrambling.

**6.** Divide the congee among 4 bowls. Let people add their own toppings and mix them in before eating.

## » CRUMPET FRENCH TOAST

MAKES 2 SERVINGS

2 large eggs
Freshly ground black pepper
    to taste
2 crumpets
1 tsp (5 mL) unsalted butter
Minced fresh red or green
    chilies to taste (optional)
Pure maple syrup, warmed,
    for serving

Thanks to our British ties, Canadians still adore crumpets, those soft, spongy and yeasty rounds with holes on the top. We usually just toast and butter them, but this Jamie Oliver idea is more creative. Jamie often visits Toronto on book tours and I've interviewed him several times, feeding him moose steaks and burgers once, and watching him make pancakes with the kids at the Stop Community Food Centre another time. Jamie likes to serve this with bacon which he fries first so he can use the drippings to cook the crumpets.

**1.** In a shallow dish, whisk together the eggs and pepper. Soak the crumpets in the eggs for about 30 seconds per side.

**2.** In a medium non-stick skillet, melt the butter over medium heat. Add the crumpets, holey side down, to the skillet. Cook until golden, about 4 minutes. Flip the crumpets and cook until the undersides are golden, about 4 minutes.

**3.** Serve sprinkled with chilies, if desired, and drizzled with maple syrup.

"Since we're all breakfasters, I passed this recipe on to my nephews and brother. Also, oatmeal is heart-smart as it reduces cholesterol."

**KATIE CLOUGH,** COBOURG, ONT.

In a 2008 story called "Haute oats," I celebrated the rise of chewy oatmeal made from steel-cut oats, the fibre-rich whole oats that are cut into thirds instead of being rolled and flattened into flakes. Toronto chef Jamie Kennedy serves steel-cut oatmeal at Gilead Café (jamiekennedy.ca), and also makes it for the Porridge for Parkinson's fundraiser, topping it with ¼ ounce of Scotch whisky if requested. This version is an amalgamation of everything I've learned about oatmeal. For a creamier porridge, use 3 cups (750 mL) water and 1 cup (250 mL) milk.

## TOASTED STEEL-CUT OATMEAL

READERS' CHOICE

MAKES ABOUT 4 SERVINGS

1 tbsp (15 mL) unsalted butter
1 cup (250 mL) steel-cut oats
4 cups (1 L) water
¼ cup (60 mL) raisins and/or
  dried cranberries (optional)
¼ tsp (1 mL) kosher salt
  (optional)
Pure maple syrup, warmed,
  for serving (optional)

**1.** In a medium skillet, melt the butter over medium heat. When it begins to foam, add the oats, then cook, stirring constantly, until the oats are golden and fragrant, about 2 minutes. Set aside.

**2.** In a medium saucepan, bring the water to a gentle simmer over medium heat. Add the toasted oats and raisins and/or cranberries (if using). Simmer, uncovered, without stirring, until the mixture thickens, about 20 minutes. Stir lightly and add salt (if using).

**3.** Continue to simmer until the oats have absorbed most of the liquid and are tender but still slightly chewy, about 5 minutes.

**4.** Remove the saucepan from the heat and let stand, uncovered, for 5 to 10 minutes to thicken.

**5.** Stir well then spoon into individual bowls and serve drizzled with warm maple syrup, if desired. Refrigerate any leftovers in an airtight container. Reheat by spooning each portion into a small bowl, adding a splash of water, then microwaving for 60 to 90 seconds.

## » MAPLE-QUINOA PORRIDGE

MAKES 2 SERVINGS

2 cups (500 mL) water
1 cup (250 mL) dried quinoa, rinsed
10 cardamom pods
¼ cup (60 mL) pure maple syrup
1 tsp (5 mL) ground cinnamon
8 dried apricots, finely diced
4 dried figs, stemmed and finely diced
¼ cup (60 mL) milk (optional), plus more if desired
¼ cup (60 mL) slivered almonds

I did a three-year stint as a brunch columnist and this recipe was one of my favourite discoveries in 2006. Sasha Chan made this porridge at Le Café Vert, an organic bistro that's since closed. Quinoa, which has been dubbed "vegetarian caviar," is a nutty, grain-like seed and complete protein that worked its way from South America to North American health food stores and into mainstream supermarkets. Feel free to boost the dried fruit or add fresh berries.

**1.** In a medium saucepan, combine the water, quinoa and cardamom pods. Bring to a boil over high heat, then reduce the heat to medium-low. Simmer, covered, until the water is almost all absorbed, about 12 minutes.

**2.** Stir in the maple syrup and cinnamon, then simmer, uncovered, for 2 minutes. Discard the cardamom pods, then stir in the apricots, figs and ¼ cup (60 mL) milk (if using).

**3.** Remove from the heat and let stand, covered, for about 10 minutes. Stir well then spoon into individual bowls and serve garnished with almonds. If needed, thin with a little additional milk.

*Right: Red, white and black quinoa*

## » DESIGN-YOUR-OWN GREEK YOGURT

MAKES 1 SERVING

½ cup (125 mL) plain
    Greek yogurt

**Toppings**
Liquid honey, pure maple syrup
    or agave nectar
Fresh berries (blueberries,
    raspberries, chopped
    strawberries)
Fresh fruit (chopped bananas,
    apples or pears)
Dried fruit (quartered figs,
    halved Medjool dates,
    chopped apricots)
Nuts (almonds, pecans, walnuts)
Jam or jelly (raspberry, fig,
    apricot)
Chocolate chips or grated
    chocolate
Granola

I was exploring Queens in New York City when I discovered a takeout shop serving thick Greek yogurt with an array of toppings like nuts, honey, dried fruit, cooked fruit and sour cherry sauce. I'm still waiting for a Toronto entrepreneur to seize on the idea, but in the meantime, Greek yogurt has become the next superfood. Not all Greek (or "Greek-style") yogurts are created equal so do a taste test (if your spoon stands up, you've probably found a good one). My preferred brands are Greek Gods, Fage and Chobani.

This is my favourite kind of recipe, meaning it's an idea and a set of flavour combinations rather than a strict recipe. This could be a quick breakfast for one or, if you use more yogurt, a dessert for a family supper or dinner party.

**1.** Put yogurt in a serving bowl and stir well. Add whatever toppings you like.

Frank Jones may have been an award-winning, globe-trotting *Star* reporter, but he's revered in food circles for the annual column he wrote in the 1980s and 1990s about his wife, Ayesha's, Seville orange marmalade. The bitter, thick-skinned, seedy oranges appear briefly in select supermarkets in January and February. But Frank only wrote about the marmalade in narrative form, so I went to his home to watch Ayesha make a batch.

# SEVILLE ORANGE MARMALADE «

MAKES ABOUT 12 CUPS (3 L)

8 Seville oranges, washed and dried (about 3 lb/1.3 kg)
12 cups (3 L) water
9 cups (2.25 mL) granulated sugar

**1.** Cut each orange in half and remove and reserve the seeds. Slice the oranges (skin, pulp and pith) as thinly as possible. Wrap the seeds in a small piece of cheesecloth and tie with kitchen twine to form a bag (their pectin helps to set the marmalade).

**2.** Put the oranges and seed bag in a large bowl with the water. Cover the bowl with a clean tea towel and let stand at room temperature for 2 to 3 days, stirring occasionally.

**3.** For the first boil, tip the orange mixture into a very large, heavy-bottomed pot and bring to a boil over high heat. Reduce the heat to low, then simmer, uncovered, until the orange peel is very soft, 1 to 2 hours, depending on the thickness of your slices. Carefully tip the contents of the pot back into the large bowl and let to cool to room temperature.

**4.** For the second boil, spoon 4 cups (1 L) orange mixture back into the pot and add 3 cups (750 mL) sugar. (The marmalade needs to be cooked in 3 batches or it won't set.) Bring to a boil over high heat, then reduce the heat to medium and simmer gently, uncovered, stirring often, until the mixture foams, thickens and reaches the gel stage, about 15 to 20 minutes.

**5.** To test if the marmalade is ready, spoon a little onto a small chilled plate and put it in the fridge. If, after a few minutes, you can see that a skin has formed on the surface when you nudge it with your finger, it's ready. Alternatively, dip a cool, metal spoon into the marmalade, then remove and jiggle the spoon. If the mixture falls from the spoon in sheets, it's ready.

**6.** Remove the pot from the heat and let cool for 5 minutes. Remove the seed bag and reserve it for boiling the remaining batches of marmalade. Ladle the marmalade into hot, sterilized Mason jars or other glass containers. Seal, then refrigerate for up to 1 month.

**7.** Repeat the boiling process twice with the remaining orange mixture and sugar. (If you have 3 pots, you can boil all 3 batches at once.)

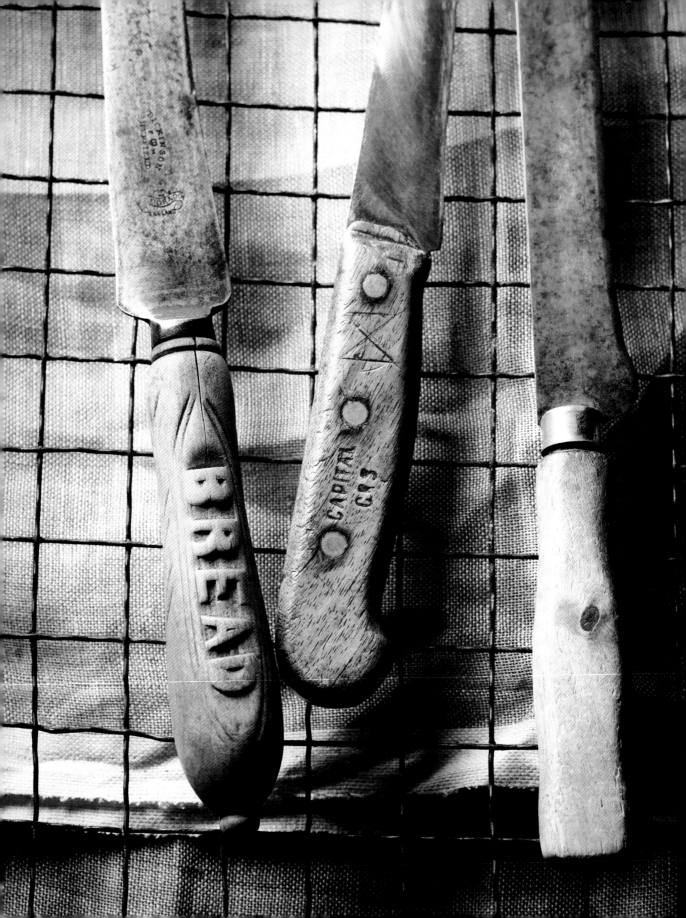

# DIPS, SNACKS, BREADS AND SANDWICHES

A celebration of loosely related recipes for things you eat with bread, things you spread on bread (and crackers), and the breads themselves.

## » HABEEB'S BABAGHANOUJ

MAKES ABOUT 3 CUPS (750 ML)

2 lb (900 g) Italian eggplants (about 2 medium), pierced all over with a fork
¼ cup (60 mL) well-stirred tahini (sesame paste)
¼ cup (60 mL) fresh lemon juice
¼ cup (60 mL) extra virgin olive oil
2 large cloves garlic, minced
1 tsp (5 mL) kosher salt
½ tsp (2 mL) freshly ground black pepper
¼ tsp (1 mL) ground cumin
¼ tsp (1 mL) ground coriander
Pita bread for serving

Like hummus, babaghanouj is a Middle Eastern dish that tastes way better if you make your own. It's usually eaten as a dip, but you can add it to sandwiches or wraps, or serve it alongside main dishes like grilled meats or the Portobello-Quinoa Stacks on page 158, or with rice. This rustic version comes from Toronto food writer Habeeb Salloum, who included it in *The Arabian Nights Cookbook* (Tuttle Publishing, 2010). He mashes this by hand, but I find puréeing it in a food processor gives it a silkier texture.

**1.** Preheat the oven to 425°F (220°C). Put the eggplants on a rimmed baking sheet or in a large baking dish. Bake in the oven, turning often with tongs, until they feel soft when a knife is inserted in the flesh, about 60 minutes. Let cool for about 15 minutes.

**2.** When the eggplants are cool enough to handle, trim and discard the ends, and peel off and discard the skin. Transfer the eggplant pulp, seeds and juices to a medium bowl.

**3.** For a rustic babaghanouj, mash the eggplant pulp to the desired texture with a potato masher or fork. In a small bowl, stir together the tahini, lemon juice, oil, garlic, salt, pepper, cumin and coriander. Add to the eggplant and mash well.

**4.** For a smooth babaghanouj, combine the eggplant pulp, seeds and juices, tahini, lemon juice, oil, garlic, salt, pepper, cumin and coriander in a food processor and purée until smooth.

**5.** Spread the babaghanouj out on a platter and serve warm or at room temperature with wedges of pita bread, or refrigerate it in a airtight container for up to 5 days.

## » MY FAVOURITE HUMMUS

MAKES ABOUT 2 CUPS (500 ML)

1 can (19 oz/540 mL) chickpeas, drained and rinsed
6 tbsp (90 mL) fresh lemon juice (from about 2 lemons)
¼ cup (60 mL) well-stirred tahini (sesame paste)
3 large cloves garlic, minced
1 tsp (5 mL) kosher salt
¼ tsp (1 mL) cayenne or paprika
¼ tsp (1 mL) freshly ground black pepper
¼ tsp (1 mL) tamari or soy sauce
Water, if needed

Hummus, the universally loved chickpea and tahini dip, should be in everybody's kitchen arsenal. I like mine to be assertive, and serve it as a dip with the Za'atar Pita Chips (page 44) or raw vegetables, spread it in sandwiches or slather some on my Portobello-Quinoa Stacks (page 158). Tahini can be thin and pourable or thick and pasty, depending on the brand. I prefer the kind that can be easily drizzled.

**1.** In a food processor, combine the chickpeas, lemon juice, tahini, garlic, salt, cayenne or paprika, black pepper and tamari or soy sauce, then purée until smooth. For a thinner or smoother dip, continue to purée, adding water 1 tbsp (15 mL) at a time, until the dip is the desired consistency.

**2.** Serve immediately or refrigerate in an airtight container for up to 5 days.

## FETA AND OREGANO DIP

MAKES ABOUT ½ CUP (125 ML)

½ cup (125 mL) crumbled feta cheese
¼ cup (60 mL) fruity extra virgin olive oil, plus more if needed
2 tsp (10 mL) dried oregano leaves
Pita or other bread for serving

Gokhan Gokyilmaz and Su Goral, whose Turkish olive oil, Zei (zeioliveoil.com), is sold in fine food stores across Ontario, made this three-ingredient dip for me during an olive oil tasting at their Toronto home. They served it with fresh bread, Arbequina olives, an avocado and tomato salad, and a spicy walnut and feta dip called muhammara.

**1.** In a medium bowl, combine the feta and ¼ cup (60 mL) oil. Sprinkle with oregano, crumbling the herb between your fingers, then mash well with a fork. The dip should be quite loose and very yellow. If not, drizzle with more oil.

**2.** Serve immediately with pita or other bread, or refrigerate in an airtight container for up to 2 days.

Everyone should know how to fix homemade guac. Hass avocados (the ones with the knobbly skin), white onions and cilantro are key but sometimes I skip the tomatoes. Occasionally I follow actress/cookbook author Eva Longoria's lead, dice the avocados, instead of mashing them, and add a splash of lemon juice. For extra heat, do what Toronto-based Mexican chef Francisco Alejandri does and use Scotch bonnet or habanero chilies with their seeds. This is great with homemade corn chips: cut fresh corn tortillas into wedges and fry them in canola oil over medium heat until crisp.

**1.** In a medium bowl, combine the avocados, tomato, cilantro, onion, jalapeño or chilies and lime juice. Mash with a fork to the desired texture. Taste, and add salt and more lime juice, if desired.

**2.** Serve the guacamole immediately, with tortilla chips, or press plastic wrap directly on the surface so the guacamole doesn't brown, then refrigerate it for up to 6 hours.

# GO-TO GUACAMOLE

《

MAKES ABOUT 2 CUPS (500 ML)

2 Hass avocados, peeled and pitted
1 plum (roma) tomato, seeded and chopped
½ cup (125 mL) chopped cilantro
⅓ cup (80 mL) finely chopped white onion
1 large jalapeño pepper or 2 fresh serrano or other small green chilies, with seeds, minced
Juice of 1 lime, plus more if needed
½ tsp (2 mL) kosher salt, or to taste
Tortilla chips, for serving

## » ERIC VELLEND'S HOMEMADE RICOTTA

### READERS' CHOICE

MAKES ABOUT 1-¼ CUPS
(310 ML)

3-½ cups (875 mL)
    homogenized (3.25%) milk
½ cup (125 mL) whipping cream
½ tsp (2 mL) kosher salt
2 tbsp (30 mL) white wine
    vinegar

"Who would have thought making a cheese could be this embarrassingly easy?!"

**MARY PRAWECKI,** WIARTON, ONT.

It takes just four ingredients to make ricotta, a fresh, moist, slightly sweet cheese that's lovely on its own, drizzled with extra virgin olive oil and flaky sea salt, or topped with honey. Freelance writer Eric Vellend's version can be served with baguette slices or grilled or toasted bread, but he also recommends dolloping it on spaghetti tossed with pesto or tomato sauce.

**1.** Cut 2 pieces of cheesecloth, each large enough to line a fine-mesh sieve. Moisten the pieces of cheesecloth with water, squeeze them dry and line the sieve with the cheesecloth, making a double layer. Set the sieve over a medium bowl.

**2.** In a medium saucepan, combine the milk, cream and salt. Bring to a slow boil over medium heat, stirring occasionally with a wooden spoon. When the mixture starts to boil, stir in the vinegar, then remove from the heat. Let stand for 2 minutes, then pour the mixture into the prepared sieve.

**3.** For wet ricotta, let stand for 5 minutes, then discard the whey that has accumulated in the bowl. For firmer ricotta, let stand for 20 to 45 minutes (depending on how firm a cheese you want), then discard the whey.

**4.** Serve immediately either spread on a platter or piled in a bowl. Alternatively, refrigerate in an airtight container for up to 3 days.

I stumbled on this unusual salsa at the Royal Agricultural Winter Fair in 2002 and haven't seen anything like it since. It was created by Sudbury chef Tom Reid at FedNor's Northern Ontario Agriculture and Food Exhibition. Tom still sells this through his gourmet food company Vinegar on the Rocks (vinegarontherocks.ca).

**1.** Trim and discard the end from the orange half and cut the orange half into 2 pieces. In a food processor, combine the orange pieces and ginger, then process for 1 minute. Transfer to a bowl.

**2.** Add the cranberries to the food processor, then pulse until coarsely chopped. Add the cranberries to the orange mixture.

**3.** Stir in the raisins, 2 tbsp (30 mL) sugar, 2 tbsp (30 mL) honey and the chilies (if using). Cover and refrigerate for at least 1 hour or up to 1 day to let the flavours develop.

**4.** Just before serving, stir in the cheese. Taste and, if a sweeter salsa is desired, add a little more sugar or honey. Serve with tortilla chips or crackers for dipping.

# CRANBERRY-ORANGE SALSA

《

MAKES ABOUT 2-½ CUPS (625 ML)

½ seedless orange with peel, washed
1 tbsp (15 mL) minced crystallized ginger
2 cups (500 mL) fresh or frozen and thawed cranberries
½ cup (125 mL) raisins (preferably golden)
2 tbsp (30 mL) granulated sugar, or more to taste
2 tbsp (30 mL) liquid honey, or more to taste
2 tsp (10 mL) minced and seeded fresh red chilies (optional)
3 oz (85 g) chèvre (soft unripened goat cheese), crumbled
Tortilla chips or crackers for serving

## ZA'ATAR PITA CHIPS

MAKES 16

1 large (9-inch/23 cm) whole
     wheat pita pocket
2 tbsp (30 mL) za'atar
     (spice blend)
¼ cup (60 mL) extra virgin olive
     oil

This is how I transform slightly stale pita into something fabulous. Za'atar is an intoxicating Middle Eastern herb blend that usually combines dried wild thyme, roasted sesame seeds, ground sumac and salt. I buy mine in bags from Middle Eastern shops such as Arz Fine Foods (arzbakery.com), but it's becoming more accessible and there's even a President's Choice za'atar now.

Za'atar is also great sprinkled on hummus or scrambled eggs, or you can mix it with extra virgin olive oil and paint it onto any flatbread, like naan, with a silicone pastry brush.

**1.** Preheat the oven to 350°F (180°C). Using scissors, carefully split the pita horizontally into two thin rounds, then cut each round into 8 wedges.

**2.** Arrange the wedges on a large baking sheet, rough (inside) sides facing up. Sprinkle each piece with za'atar, then drizzle each with oil.

**3.** Bake in the oven until crisp and golden, 5 to 6 minutes. Serve warm or let cool completely on a wire rack. Store in an airtight container at room temperature for up to 2 days.

I discovered Diva Q (Danielle Dimovski) at the Canadian Pork BBQ Championships in Paris, Ontario, in 2007 and wrote a story about her called "Chicks in the pit." Danielle fed me the barbecued version of these ABTs ("atomic buffalo turds" in barbecue circles, but don't let the name put you off) and I ate a shameful number of them. The 2007 event was the Barrie mom's first stab at competitive barbecuing. In 2011, Danielle (divaq.ca) was named world champion in the pork category in the Jack Daniel's World Championship Invitational Barbecue in Tennessee.

# DIVA Q'S CHEESY ABTS ≪

MAKES 20

Half 250 g package cream
    cheese (4 oz/125 g), at room
    temperature
¼ cup (60 mL) coarsely grated
    smoked mozzarella cheese
¼ cup (60 mL) finely grated
    Parmigiano Reggiano
2 tbsp (30 mL) finely grated
    Romano cheese
2 tbsp (30 mL) finely diced
    yellow onion
1 tsp (5 mL) pure ancho or
    chipotle chili powder
1 tsp (5 mL) hot sauce
¼ tsp (1 mL) garlic powder or
    1 clove garlic, minced
10 large jalapeño peppers,
    seeded and halved
    lengthwise, stems left intact
20 slices bacon

**1.** Preheat the oven to 350°F (180°C). Grease a large rimmed baking sheet and set a large wire rack on top.

**2.** In a medium bowl, combine the cream cheese, mozzarella, Parmigiano Reggiano, Romano, onion, chili powder, hot sauce and garlic. Mash well with a potato masher, fork or wooden spoon until the mixture is smooth and the ingredients are well combined.

**3.** Generously spoon the cheese mixture into the jalapeño halves, using about 1 tbsp (15 mL) for large jalapeños, less for smaller ones. Tightly wrap 1 slice of bacon around each jalapeño half. (If you have any of the cheese mixture left over, use it to make more bacon-wrapped jalapeños or refrigerate it for another use, such as a sandwich filling.)

**4.** Arrange the wrapped jalapeños in a single layer on the rack on the prepared baking sheet.

**5.** Bake in the oven until the bacon is crisp, the cheese is bubbling out of the edges and the jalapeño stems can be pulled out easily, 45 to 60 minutes. Let cool for 10 minutes before serving.

## » DEVILS ON HORSEBACK

MAKES 12

12 Medjool dates
3 oz (85 g) Monforte Paradiso
   cheese, cut into 12 pieces
6 strips bacon, patted dry and
   cut crosswise in half
12 wooden toothpicks

I love the name of this classic hot appetizer. It usually involves prunes or dates stuffed with cheese, chutney, almonds or smoked oysters, then wrapped in bacon. This version comes from chef Matty Matheson of Parts & Labour restaurant (partsandlabour. ca). It doubles easily if you're feeding a crowd. At the restaurant, which boasts a contemporary Canadian menu, Matty uses Paradiso, a buttery, aged washed-rind sheep's milk cheese from Monforte Dairy (monfortedairy.com) in Stratford. Some cheesemongers sell it, or you could substitute Italian Taleggio or fontina, or even brie or Camembert.

**1.** Preheat the oven to 450°F (230°C). Make a lengthwise slit in each date and remove the pits. Stuff each date with 1 piece of cheese, then form each date back into its original shape. Wrap each date tightly in a piece of bacon.

**2.** Heat an ovenproof non-stick skillet over medium heat. Add the dates, seam sides down, and cook until the bacon is crisp on the undersides, about 3 minutes. Flip the dates and cook until the other side is crisp, about 2 minutes. Transfer the skillet to the oven and bake for 3 minutes.

**3.** Remove the dates to a paper-towel-lined plate to drain briefly. Skewer each on a toothpick and arrange on a serving platter.

This sensational spicy-sweet relish is the creation of John Butler, head chef of St. Joseph's Health Centre. He dazzles cafeteria-goers with his locally minded menu and daily specials. He dollops this relish on his Bison Burgers with Smoked Gouda (page 110), but you can use it however you like—on sandwiches, with eggs, or alongside any meat, poultry or fish.

## RED PEPPER RELISH ≪

MAKES ABOUT 4 CUPS (1 L)

5 red bell peppers, seeded and finely chopped
4 jalapeño peppers, seeded, if desired, and finely chopped
2 tart apples (such as McIntosh), peeled, cored and chopped
1-½ cups (375 mL) granulated sugar
1-½ cups (375 mL) cider vinegar
1 tbsp (15 mL) kosher salt
¼ cup (60 mL) chopped cilantro

**1.** In a large saucepan, combine the bell peppers, jalapeño peppers, apples, sugar, vinegar and salt, and bring to a boil over high heat. Reduce the heat to medium and simmer briskly, uncovered, until thickened and reduced to about 4 cups (1 L), 35 to 45 minutes.

**2.** Remove the saucepan from the heat and let cool for 10 minutes. Stir in the cilantro. Let cool completely then refrigerate in an airtight container for up to 2 weeks.

I love the homemade coconut chutneys in Indian restaurants as much as I hate the ones you can buy in jars. Geetha Upadhyaya showed me how to make my own when I went to her Scarborough house to watch her cook a weeknight family meal for my *What's for Dinner* series. South Asian grocery stores sell small bags of frozen, finely grated coconut. Tamarind concentrate is much thicker than tamarind sauce. I like the Tamcon brand.

**1.** In a small non-stick skillet over medium heat, combine the chilies, dal and ghee. Toast, stirring occasionally and reducing the heat if necessary, until lightly browned and fragrant, about 5 minutes.

**2.** Transfer the mixture to a food processor and add the salt. Process until finely minced. Add the coconut, ½ cup (125 mL) water and the tamarind concentrate, then process until smooth. If the chutney seems too thick, add a little more water and process again.

**3.** Serve at room temperature. Refrigerate in an airtight container for up to 1 day. Return it to room temperature before serving.

# COCONUT AND RED CHILI CHUTNEY ≪

MAKES ABOUT ¾ CUP (185 ML)

2 finger-length dried red chilies (preferably Kashmiri)
1 tsp (5 mL) white urad dal (skinned, split urad lentils), rinsed
½ tsp (2 mL) ghee (clarified butter)
½ tsp (2 mL) fine sea salt
¾ cup (185 mL) finely grated fresh coconut (thawed if frozen)
½ cup (125 mL) water, plus more if needed
¼ tsp (1 mL) tamarind concentrate

*Left: Dried pequín (in bowl) and Kashmiri chilies*

## » QUINN'S SODA BREAD

MAKES 1 LOAF

1-½ cups (375 mL) whole
  wheat flour
1-½ cups (375 mL) all-purpose
  flour
¼ cup (60 mL) granulated
  sugar
1 tbsp (15 mL) baking powder
1 tsp (5 mL) baking soda
1 tsp (5 mL) kosher salt
2 cups (500 mL) lightly shaken
  buttermilk
1 large egg
¼ cup (60 mL) unsalted
  butter, melted and cooled
  slightly
¼ cup (60 mL) large-flake oats

This traditional Irish quick bread is made with baking soda and baking powder instead of yeast, and I like it because there's no kneading. Paul Pisa, executive chef of Quinn's Steakhouse & Irish Bar (quinnssteakhouse.com), created it for his breadbasket and showed me how to make it for a St. Patrick's Day story in 2010. He serves it buttered with smoked salmon, thin rings of red onion, capers and lemon juice.

**1.** Preheat the oven to 325°F (160°F). Grease a large baking sheet. In a medium mixing bowl, whisk together the whole wheat and all-purpose flours, sugar, baking powder, baking soda and salt. Make a well in the centre.

**2.** In a measuring cup or bowl, beat together the buttermilk and egg. Pour the buttermilk mixture into the well in the flour mixture, then mix with rubber spatula just until the dry ingredients are moistened.

**3.** Add the butter, then mix with the spatula or your hands, until all the ingredients are incorporated. The dough will be sticky and wet.

**4.** Tip the dough (it will be very loose) onto the prepared baking sheet and gently pat into an 8-inch (20 cm) round. Using a wet knife, cut a deep cross in the top of the loaf, then sprinkle generously with oats.

**5.** Bake in the centre of the oven until brown and crusty on top, and a cake tester inserted in the centre comes out clean, 65 to 70 minutes.

**6.** Let the loaf cool on a wire rack. Serve warm cut into slices. When completely cold, store the bread in a cotton bag for up to 2 days.

Freelance writer Corey Mintz (porkosity.blogspot.com) got this from Cory Vitiello, chef at The Harbord Room (theharbordroom .com), for a 2009 story on school lunches. The chef has tweaked it since, adding green onions, cilantro and the bacon/chorizo option. Use any brand of fine cornmeal, but Cory prefers Bob's Red Mill for the coarse cornmeal (look for it in the natural food area of most supermarkets).

**1.** Preheat the oven to 350°F (180°C). Grease a 9- x 13-inch (23 x 33 cm) baking dish.

**2.** In a medium non-stick skillet, heat the oil over medium heat. If using bacon, add it to the skillet and cook until lightly browned, about 5 minutes. If using chorizo, remove it from its casing, crumble into the skillet and cook until lightly browned, about 5 minutes. Add the yellow onion and jalapeño, then cook, stirring, for 10 minutes. Set aside.

**3.** In a large bowl, whisk together the flour, coarse cornmeal, sugar, fine cornmeal, baking powder and salt. Add the onion mixture, corn, green onion and cilantro, and stir well with a wooden spoon.

**4.** In a small bowl, whisk the eggs, then whisk in the buttermilk and butter. Add the egg mixture to the flour mixture and mix just until the dry ingredients are moistened.

**5.** Pour the batter into the prepared dish. Bake in the oven until a cake tester inserted in the centre comes out fairly clean, 30 to 40 minutes. Let cool in the dish for 5 minutes before slicing as desired. Store in an airtight container at room temperature for up to 1 day.

# THE HARBORD ROOM'S CORNBREAD　《

MAKES 1 LOAF

1 tsp (5 mL) vegetable oil
½ cup (125 mL) finely diced bacon or fresh chorizo sausage (optional)
½ medium yellow onion, finely chopped
1 jalapeño pepper, seeded and finely chopped
2 cups (500 mL) all-purpose flour
1-¼ cups (310 mL) coarse whole grain cornmeal
⅓ cup (80 mL) granulated sugar
¼ cup (60 mL) fine cornmeal
2 tbsp (30 mL) baking powder
1 tsp (5 mL) kosher salt
1 cup (250 mL) fresh or frozen and thawed corn kernels
1 green onion, thinly sliced
1 tbsp (15 mL) chopped cilantro
2 large eggs
1-½ cups (375 mL) well-shaken buttermilk
2 tbsp (30 mL) unsalted butter, melted and cooled

## » LIZET'S SWEET ANISE BREAD

MAKES 1 LOAF

2 cups (500 mL) all-purpose
    flour
1 cup (250 mL) granulated sugar
1 cup (250 mL) 2% milk
1 large egg
1-½ tsp (7 mL) soft, tub
    margarine or unsalted butter
1-½ tsp (7 mL) baking powder
½ tsp (2 mL) anise seed
½ tsp (2 mL) ground cinnamon

My first real food craving was for Lizet Catita's sweet bread. Lizet cleaned our Toronto home when I was little and often treated our family to her delicious anise bread inspired by the pão doce her grandmother made in Portugal.

I dreamed of this bread for years, but never dared make it lest it not live up to my memory of it. But when I finally did test it for this book (using margarine, which was popular in the 1970s and 1980s, as Lizet did), it was exactly how I remembered it. It's dense and licorice-sweet on the inside and chewy-crisp on the outside.

**1.** Preheat the oven to 375°F (190°C). Grease a 9- x 5-inch (23 x 13 cm) loaf pan.

**2.** In a food processor, combine the flour, sugar, milk, egg, margarine or butter, baking powder, anise seed and cinnamon, and process until combined.

**3.** Pour the batter into the prepared pan. Bake in the centre of the oven until a cake tester inserted in the centre of the loaf comes out clean, 45 to 55 minutes. The bread will puff up and the top may crack. Let cool for 5 minutes in the pan, then transfer to a wire rack to cool completely.

**4.** Cut into slices to serve. Store in an airtight container at room temperature for up to 2 days.

When Pancho's Bakery (panchosbakery.ca) opened in 2009, Adalberto Aguilar and Violeta Correa showed me how to make these tortas de frijoles (Mexican pinto bean subs) using their own bolillos, long, wide, flour-dusted, white buns that are similar to crusty French rolls or kaisers.

This is a simple, vegetarian sub, but you can jazz it up by adding cooked spicy Mexican chorizo (without the casing) to the beans, or tucking some extras into the sandwich, like sliced avocado, guacamole, diced tomatoes or cilantro leaves.

# MEXICAN PINTO BEAN AND CHEESE SUBS ≪

MAKES 4

1 can (19 oz/540 mL) whole pinto beans, undrained

4 bolillo buns, crusty French rolls or Kaisers (about 8 inches/20 cm long), sliced open

About 1 cup (250 mL) coarsely grated Mexican cheese (such as Oaxaca, panela, queso fresco), mozzarella or Monterey Jack

About ¾ cup (185 mL) red or green Mexican salsa

4 drained pickled jalapeños (from a can), seeded and sliced lengthwise into thin strips or pickled jalapeño slices to taste

**1.** In a small saucepan over medium heat, cook the beans in their liquid, mashing them with a potato masher or wooden spoon, until they're quite thick and the consistency of very soft mashed potatoes, 10 to 12 minutes.

**2.** Preheat the oven to 350°F (180°C). Spread the beans evenly over the bottom half of each bun. (If desired, you can scrape out some bread from the bun bottoms and tops to make more room for the beans.) Sprinkle each with about ¼ cup (60 mL) cheese, then drizzle each with about 3 tbsp (45 mL) salsa. Divide the jalapeños among the buns, then cover with the tops of the buns.

**3.** Transfer the subs to a baking sheet. Bake in the oven until the cheese melts and the buns are slightly crispy, about 10 minutes. Let stand for 1 minute, then slice in half before serving.

## » VIETNAMESE SUBS
### (BANH MI)

MAKES 4

**Carrot-Daikon Pickle**

1 cup (250 mL) peeled and
    julienned or coarsely grated
    carrots
½ cup (125 mL) peeled and
    julienned or coarsely grated
    daikon radish
1 cup (250 mL) water
1 cup (250 mL) white vinegar
¼ cup (60 mL) granulated sugar
2 tbsp (30 mL) kosher salt

**Subs**

4 crusty but airy white buns,
    such as Kaisers or French
    rolls, or pieces of baguette
    (6 to 8 inches/15 to 20 cm
    long), sliced almost all the
    way open
Mayonnaise for spreading
Pâté (pork, chicken or mixture)
    to taste
4 long, thin slices or spears
    English cucumber (about
    5 inches/13 cm)
12 large sprigs cilantro, ends
    trimmed
Minced jalapeño pepper, with
    seeds, to taste
Freshly ground black pepper to
    taste

These subs are one of Toronto's greatest lunch deals. For about $2 you get an airy but crusty French bun filled with some form of protein (pâté, sliced deli meats, meatballs, chicken, tofu), brined carrots and daikon radishes, cilantro and chilies. In many cities, banh mi are warmed in a toaster oven, but here they're usually made to order and eaten at room temperature, so they're a cinch to make at home.

**1.** For the Carrot-Daikon Pickle, stir together the carrots and daikon in a medium bowl. In a measuring cup, stir together the water, vinegar, sugar and salt, then pour over the carrot mixture. Refrigerate, covered, for at least 1 hour or up to 1 week.

**2.** For the subs, spread inside top and bottom of each bun lightly with mayonnaise, then spread with pâté to taste.

**3.** Drain the Carrot-Daikon Pickle and pat dry on paper towels. Put a layer of Carrot-Daikon Pickle on the bottom half of each bun. Top with the cucumber and cilantro, then sprinkle with jalapeño and black pepper to taste.

Toronto's nickname, Hogtown, pays homage to our pork processing past. In a 2004 story "Welcome to Hogtown," I tried to figure out if Toronto had or even wanted to have a signature dish. Readers were vehemently divided, but many felt that the grilled peameal sandwich on a bun was a strong contender. It is a must-have at the St. Lawrence Market, where the Carousel Bakery makes an Amazing Maple condiment that inspired my mustard. You could use honey mustard.

**1.** For the Maple-Horseradish Mustard, stir together the mustard, maple syrup and horseradish in a small bowl.

**2.** For the sandwich, heat the oil in a medium cast iron or regular skillet over medium heat. Add the peameal and cook until it is lightly browned, about 3 minutes per side.

**3.** Pile the peameal onto the bottom half of the warmed bun and top with the Maple-Horseradish Mustard. Cover with the top half of the bun.

# HOGTOWN'S PEAMEAL SANDWICH

≪

MAKES 1

**Maple-Horseradish Mustard**
1 tbsp (15 mL) whole-grain mustard
2 tsp (10 mL) pure maple syrup
1 tsp (5 mL) drained prepared
 horseradish

**Sandwich**
1 tbsp (15 mL) vegetable oil
3 to 5 slices peameal bacon
 (thick or thin, as desired)
1 soft white or whole wheat
 Kaiser or other bun, warmed
 and sliced open

## » COCOA SLOPPY JOES

MAKES 4

½ cup (125 mL) ketchup
1 tbsp (15 mL) unsweetened
   cocoa powder
1 tbsp (15 mL) chili powder
1 tbsp (15 mL) prepared yellow
   mustard
½ tsp (2 mL) kosher salt
½ tsp (2 mL) freshly ground
   black pepper
12 oz (340 g) lean ground beef
1 small yellow onion, chopped
4 small, soft, whole wheat
   hamburger buns, warmed

My favourite grown-up version of sloppy joes takes its cue from the Mexican mole sauce that blends chilies and chocolate, and is adapted from a recipe created by Hershey's to promote its cocoa powder. The chili powder here refers to the readily available supermarket variety labelled "chili powder" that contains chilies, spices and garlic.

**1.** In a small bowl, stir together the ketchup, cocoa, chili powder, mustard, salt and pepper. Set aside.

**2.** In a medium non-stick skillet over medium-high heat, cook the beef and onion, stirring often, until the beef is browned and cooked through, about 10 minutes. If necessary, drain off any excess fat.

**3.** Stir the ketchup mixture into the beef mixture. Reduce the heat to low and cook, stirring often, for 5 to 10 minutes.

**4.** Divide the beef mixture among the warmed buns and serve immediately.

Tony Sabherwal and his wife, Abby, run Magic Oven (magicoven.com), a healthy pizza and pasta restaurant with five Toronto locations. Sloppy Bunjos are a spicy vegetarian Indian sandwich he created for his Magic Oven Street Food stall at the Market 707 outside the Scadding Court Community Centre.

When I made this for the paper in 2011, Abby showed me how to soak and cook dried whole yellow peas but here we've agreed on a faster version using canned chickpeas. The tea leaves and spices add flavour and colour to the filling. For zestiest results, toast and grind your own coriander and cumin seeds.

**1.** For the Bunjo Spice Mix, stir together the coriander, cumin, ginger, garlic powder, cayenne, turmeric and garam masala in a small bowl.

**2.** For the Sloppy Bunjos, stir together the chickpeas, tea leaves and Bunjo Spice Mix in a medium saucepan. Add the tomatoes and bring to a boil over high heat. Reduce the heat to low, then simmer, uncovered, stirring occasionally, until the chickpeas are heated through and the mixture is sloppy (neither too thick nor too thin), about 20 minutes. (Add a little water if the mixture is too thick.)

**3.** Spoon about one-quarter of the chickpea mixture into a small bowl. Mash well with a potato masher or a fork, then return the mashed chickpea mixture to the saucepan. Stir well. Taste and add salt if necessary.

**4.** Spoon one-quarter of the chickpea mixture onto the bottom of each bun. Garnish as desired with onion, tamarind chutney, cilantro and jalapeño, chilies or hot sauce. Replace the tops of the buns.

# MAGIC OVEN'S  《
# SLOPPY BUNJOS

MAKES 4

**Bunjo Spice Mix**
1-½ tsp (7 mL) ground
　coriander
¾ tsp (4 mL) each: ground
　cumin, ground ginger, garlic
　powder, cayenne, turmeric
　and garam masala

**Sloppy Bunjos**
1 can (19 oz/540 mL) chickpeas,
　drained and rinsed
Tea leaves from ½ tea bag
　orange pekoe tea, finely
　ground
1 cup (250 mL) bottled strained
　tomatoes (passata) or canned
　puréed tomatoes
Water as needed
Kosher salt to taste
4 small, soft hamburger or other
　buns, sliced open

**Optional toppings**
Diced red onion
Tamarind chutney
Cilantro leaves
Minced jalapeño pepper or
　green chili, seeded if desired,
　or hot sauce

## » SMOKED CHEDDAR GRILLED CHEESE WITH SRIRACHA KETCHUP

MAKES 2

**Sriracha Ketchup**
⅓ cup (80 mL) ketchup
1 tsp (5 mL) Sriracha (Asian hot
    sauce), or to taste
Pinch freshly ground black
    pepper

**Sandwiches**
¾ cup (185 mL) coarsely grated
    smoked cheddar with rind
¼ cup (60 mL) coarsely grated
    white cheddar
4 large slices sourdough bread
Salted butter, at room
    temperature, for spreading
Cracked black pepper to taste

Sure, I've been making grilled cheese my whole life but when Kevin Durkee, co-owner of Cheesewerks restaurant (cheesewerks.com), showed me how he makes them, I learned a few new tricks. Kevin grates his cheese on the large holes of a box grater or in a food processor because grated cheese melts better than slices. He favours sourdough bread because the butter melts into its pores, and he lets his sandwiches rest before cutting them, just like steaks.

Ketchup is a must with grilled cheese and Cheesewerks makes its own from scratch, so mine is a cheater's version.

**1.** For the Sriracha Ketchup, whisk together the ketchup, Sriracha and pepper in a small bowl. Set aside.

**2.** For the sandwiches, toss the 2 cheddars in a small bowl until well combined. Spread 1 side of each bread slice with butter, right to the edges. Put the slices, butter side down, on a cutting board. Loosely top 2 slices with equal portions of the grated cheese. You want the cheese layer to be about ¼ to ½ inch (6 mm to 1 cm) thick.

**3.** Sprinkle the cheese with pepper. Top each sandwich with the remaining slice of bread, buttered side up.

**4.** Heat a large cast iron or non-stick skillet over medium heat. Add the sandwiches and cook until the undersides are golden, 2 to 3 minutes. Using a spatula, carefully flip each sandwich but don't flatten them. Cook until the undersides are golden, 2 to 3 minutes.

**5.** Transfer the sandwiches to a cutting board and let stand for 1 minute before cutting so the cheese doesn't spill out. Cut each sandwich in half diagonally using a serrated knife. Serve the sandwiches with the Sriracha Ketchup.

## » KIMCHI QUESADILLAS

MAKES 4

1 tbsp (15 mL) vegetable oil, plus more if needed

2 cups (500 mL) cabbage kimchi, drained, squeezed and chopped

4 medium whole wheat or white flour tortillas (about 8 inches/20 cm)

½ cup (125 mL) cilantro leaves or 8 fresh perilla (shiso) leaves

¼ cup (60 mL) toasted sesame seeds

1 cup (250 mL) coarsely grated aged cheddar cheese

1 cup (250 mL) coarsely grated mozzarella or Monterey Jack cheese

Inspired by Roy Choi of Kogi BBQ in Los Angeles (the godfather of the kimchi taco and kimchi quesadilla craze), and Toronto chef/cooking instructor Joanne Lusted who created a healthier version of this quesadilla, this is a recipe you can play around with. Use two large tortillas per quesadilla and cut them into wedges after filling and cooking, or be decadent and double the cheese.

Look for perilla (shiso) leaves and cabbage kimchi in Asian supermarkets. My favourite brand of kimchi is Kimchi Canada from Newmarket because it's made with anchovy sauce instead of shrimp paste (which I'm allergic to).

1. In a large non-stick skillet, heat 1 tbsp (15 mL) oil over medium heat. Add the kimchi and cook, stirring, until golden and wilted, 5 to 6 minutes. Remove the skillet from the heat.

2. Lay the tortillas in a single layer on the counter. Top half of each tortilla with 2 tbsp (30 mL) cilantro or 2 perilla leaves, one-quarter of the kimchi, 1 tbsp (15 mL) sesame seeds and ¼ cup (60 mL) each cheddar and mozzarella or Monterey Jack. Fold each tortilla in half to create a semi-circle and press gently to flatten them.

3. Return the skillet to medium heat and add a little oil, if desired. Cook the quesadillas in batches, turning once, until the tortillas are golden in patches and the cheese is melted, about 2 minutes per side. Transfer to a plate and let stand for 2 minutes before serving.

This pizzaesque bagel, inspired by the margherita pizza that duplicates the colours of the Italian flag with red (tomato sauce), white (mozzarella) and green (fresh basil), was created by freelance writer Eric Vellend.

Eric favours Gryfe's Bagel Bakery for its Jewish-style, light, plain bagels with small holes. I swear by the Montreal-style sesame bagels from The Bagel House (thebagelhouse.ca) which are dense and slightly sweet, but have large holes and so less space for the cheese. You can use a toaster oven or regular oven to cook these bagels, but they'll get crisper in the toaster oven.

**1.** Preheat the toaster oven to 375°F (190°C) and line the baking pan insert with parchment paper. Alternatively, preheat the oven to 400°F (200°C) and line a baking sheet with parchment paper.

**2.** Spread each bagel half with 1 tbsp (15 mL) tomato sauce. Top each with bocconcini, cut to fit over the bread part of the bagel and avoiding the hole.

**3.** Bake until the cheese starts to melt, about 8 minutes. Sprinkle with basil and salt before serving.

# MARGHERITA PIZZA BAGELS 《

MAKES 2 SERVINGS

1 bagel, halved
2 tbsp (30 mL) All-Purpose Tomato Sauce (page 181) or purchased tomato sauce
2 small balls bocconcini (semi-soft unripened cheese), patted dry
Torn fresh basil leaves to taste
Flaky sea salt to taste

When Kim Honey took over as food editor during my maternity leave in 2008/2009, she visited Guelph to write about Borealis Grille & Bar (borealisgrille.ca) where owner Bob Desautels challenged his chefs to source 95 per cent of the menu from Ontario. At the time, the "relentlessly local" restaurant (which is part of the Neighbourhood Group of Companies) served this flatbread with Ontario bison, and you can still find it on the menu from time to time.

# TRUE NORTH FLATBREAD «

MAKES 2 (6-8 SERVINGS)

2 tbsp (30 mL) canola oil

2 cups (500 mL) thinly sliced, halved yellow onions

2 cups (500 mL) thinly sliced white, cremini or shiitake mushrooms

4 cloves garlic, minced

8 oz (225 g) ground bison, beef, pork or sausage (removed from its casing)

1 bag (about 26 oz/737 g) fresh (or frozen and thawed in fridge) pizza dough

All-purpose flour for dusting

1 cup (250 mL) All-Purpose Tomato Sauce (page 181) or purchased tomato sauce

1 cup (250 mL) coarsely grated mozzarella

½ cup (125 mL) coarsely grated smoked cheddar

1 tbsp (15 mL) finely chopped flat-leaf parsley

**1.** In a large non-stick skillet, heat the oil over medium heat. Add the onions, mushrooms and garlic, and cook, stirring often and reducing the heat if necessary, until the onions are well browned, 10 to 15 minutes.

**2.** Meanwhile, in a medium non-stick skillet over medium heat, cook the meat, breaking it up with a wooden spoon, until it is cooked through, 6 to 8 minutes. Drain off the fat, if desired. Preheat the oven to 425°F (220°C). Oil a large baking sheet.

**3.** Roll the pizza dough in flour and divide it in half. On a lightly floured surface, roll each piece into an oval, about 14 x 8 inches (35 x 20 cm). It's okay if they're misshapen. Put each flatbread on the prepared baking sheet and prick all over with a fork to reduce blistering and puffing.

**4.** Spread ½ cup (125 mL) tomato sauce on each flatbread. Sprinkle each with half of the mozzarella, then half of the meat, half of the onion-mushroom mixture and finally half of the smoked cheddar.

**5.** Bake in the centre of the oven until the flatbread is cooked and the cheese has melted, about 14 minutes, depending on the thickness of the dough. Sprinkle with the parsley and cut into wedges to serve.

# SOUPS

> Soup is always nourishing and can often be a meal in itself.

*Left: Daikon and red radishes*

# » O&B CANTEEN'S WATERMELON GAZPACHO

## Ⓡⓔⓐⓓⓔⓡⓢ' Ⓒⓗⓞⓘⓒⓔ

MAKES ABOUT 4 SERVINGS

1 tsp (5 mL) extra virgin olive oil
1 stalk celery, peeled and thinly
    sliced
1 shallot, thinly sliced
1 tsp (5 mL) peeled, minced
    ginger
2 tbsp (30 mL) rice wine vinegar
Juice of 1-½ limes
12 cilantro leaves
8 basil leaves
6 mint leaves
4 cups (1 L) diced peeled,
    seedless watermelon
2 cups (500 mL) diced vine-
    ripened tomatoes
½ cup (125 mL) seeded and
    diced red bell pepper
Kosher salt and freshly ground
    black pepper to taste
Red or green hot sauce to taste

"I wasn't sure I wanted to try this recipe, but I was entertaining some of my friends for dinner so I took the leap and made it. I told no one what it was and they all loved it. What an impression it made in my bouillon cups! So pretty."

**CAROL JEROME**, PICKERING, ONT.

Put watermelon into a chef's hands and here's what happens: sublime gazpacho. Jason Bangerter, executive chef of O&B Canteen and Luma (which are part of the Oliver & Bonacini Restaurants empire, oliverbonacini.com), uses this as the springboard for multiple dishes including a shooter, cocktail base, sorbet and seafood sauce. My vote goes for the straightforward cold soup. The chef strains his for a refined presentation but you don't have to.

**1.** In a small saucepan, heat the oil over medium-low heat. Add the celery, shallot and ginger, and cook, stirring often, until the celery and shallot are tender and translucent, about 8 minutes. Be careful not to let the vegetables brown. Add the vinegar and lime juice and remove the saucepan from the heat.

**2.** Stack the cilantro, basil and mint leaves and tie them together with kitchen twine. Add the herb bundle to the saucepan.

**3.** Return the saucepan to medium-low heat and simmer for 2 minutes so the flavours can blend. Remove the saucepan from the heat and let stand for 15 minutes.

**4.** Remove the herb bundle from the saucepan and, when cool enough to handle, squeeze the juices from it into the saucepan, then discard the bundle.

**5.** In a large bowl, stir together the celery mixture, watermelon, tomatoes and bell pepper. In a blender or a food processor, purée the celery mixture, in batches, until relatively smooth, 1 to 2 minutes per batch.

**6.** Refrigerate in a covered container until chilled. Taste and season with salt, pepper and hot sauce if necessary.

# » GARLICKY LENTIL AND TOMATO SOUP

## READERS' CHOICE

MAKES ABOUT 6 SERVINGS

3 tbsp (45 mL) canola oil

Minced cloves from 1 head garlic

¼ cup (60 mL) chopped cilantro

1 red or green chili (about 3 inches/7.5 cm), seeded, if desired, and minced

1 can (28 oz/796 mL) stewed whole or diced tomatoes

1 tsp (5 mL) ground cumin

1 tsp (5 mL) freshly ground black pepper

6 cups (1.5 L) water

¾ cup (185 mL) brown or green lentils, rinsed

Kosher salt to taste

"My all-time favourite soup, which I make every two to three weeks during the winter. Dee-licious and healthy, too."

**CAROL BLINOV,** BEAVERTON, ONT.

Thank Toronto food writer Habeeb Salloum for this low-cost, high-flavour soup. He's from Syria but grew up on a Saskatchewan farm in the 1920s and 1930s, where his family survived on lentils and other pulses. Read the whole story in *Arab Cooking on a Saskatchewan Homestead* (Canadian Plains Research Center Press, 2005).

Canned stewed tomatoes are peeled and cooked with onions, celery and bell peppers. Use regular whole or diced canned tomatoes (and add your own veggies) if you prefer.

**1.** In a large pot, heat the oil over medium heat. Add the garlic, cilantro and chili, and cook, stirring, for 5 minutes.

**2.** Add the tomatoes and bring to a simmer, breaking up the tomatoes with a wooden spoon. Simmer, stirring occasionally, for 10 minutes. Stir in the cumin and pepper.

**3.** Add the water and lentils. Increase the heat to high and bring to a boil. Reduce the heat to medium-low, then cook, uncovered, stirring occasionally, until the lentils are tender, 30 to 40 minutes. Taste and add salt if necessary.

Ravi Kanagarajah, widely considered a soup genius, is the man behind RaviSoups (ravisoup.com). He shared this flavour-packed vegetarian recipe whose secret is its simplicity.

1. In a large pot, heat the oil over medium heat. Add the onions and cook, stirring often, until golden, 7 to 9 minutes. Reduce the heat to medium-low and add the garlic and ginger. Cook, stirring, for 2 minutes. Add the curry powder and cook, stirring, for 1 minute.

2. Add the water, lentils, apricots and tomato. Increase the heat to high and bring to a boil. Reduce the heat to medium-low and simmer, uncovered, stirring occasionally, until the apricots are very soft, about 30 minutes.

3. Using a handheld immersion blender in the pot (or in batches in a blender or food processor), purée the soup until smooth.

4. Return the soup to the pot if necessary, stir in the coconut milk and reheat over low heat without boiling, about 2 minutes. Season with salt and pepper if necessary.

5. Ladle into bowls and garnish, if desired, with a dollop of yogurt or crème fraîche and a sprinkling of cilantro.

## CURRIED RED LENTIL AND APRICOT SOUP

MAKES ABOUT 6 SERVINGS

2 tbsp (30 mL) vegetable oil
2 medium yellow onions, chopped
¼ cup (60 mL) minced garlic
¼ cup (60 mL) peeled, minced ginger
2 tbsp (30 mL) curry powder
8 cups (2 L) water
2 cups (500 mL) dried red lentils, rinsed
1 cup (250 mL) diced dried apricots (about 22)
1 plum (roma) tomato, cored and chopped
¾ cup (185 mL) well-stirred, canned unsweetened coconut milk
Kosher salt and freshly ground black pepper to taste
Plain yogurt or crème fraîche (optional)
Chopped cilantro (optional)

## » FASOLADA

### (GREEK WHITE BEAN SOUP)

MAKES ABOUT 8 SERVINGS

8 cups (2 L) water

2 cans (each 19 oz/540 mL)
    white kidney beans, drained
    and rinsed

3 medium yellow onions,
    chopped

2 large carrots, peeled and cut in
    thick rounds

2 tomatoes, finely diced

1 stalk celery, chopped

¼ cup (60 mL) extra virgin olive
    oil

5 cloves garlic, smashed

4 bay leaves

1-½ tsp (7 mL) fine sea salt

1 tsp (5 mL) freshly ground
    black pepper

1 tsp (5 mL) dried oregano

Minced yellow onion for serving

Whole or chopped, pitted
    kalamata olives for serving

Extra virgin olive oil for serving

When the movie *My Big Fat Greek Wedding* was filming in Toronto, this is one of the dishes the crew ordered to the set from Ellas Banquet Hall & Hospitality Centre (ellas.com) which, at that time, had a restaurant in Greektown. When the executive chef showed me how to make it in 2003, he soaked dried white kidney beans overnight and then cooked them for 90 minutes before adding the vegetables, but I've streamlined things by using canned beans. Don't skimp on the garnishes, and be sure to use a fruity, flavourful olive oil.

**1.** In a large pot, combine the water, beans, chopped onions, carrots, tomatoes, celery, ¼ cup (60 mL) oil, garlic, bay leaves, salt, pepper and oregano. Bring to a boil over high heat.

**2.** Reduce the heat to medium-low and simmer, covered, stirring occasionally, until the vegetables are tender, 30 to 45 minutes. Discard the bay leaves.

**3.** To serve, ladle the soup into shallow bowls. Garnish each portion with minced onion and olives, and drizzle with oil.

I was on assignment exploring Huntsville before the G8 Summit of world leaders in 2010 when I stumbled upon this stunning soup at Soul Sistas restaurant (soulsistas.ca). Owner Lorraine Morin uses orange juice and coconut milk to give the soup unexpected layers of flavour.

# MUSKOKA SUNSHINE CARROT SOUP

《

MAKES ABOUT 8 SERVINGS

¾ cup (185 mL) unsweetened frozen concentrated orange juice
¾ cup (185 mL) water
2 tbsp (30 mL) extra virgin olive oil
2 medium yellow onions, chopped
3 cloves garlic, minced
3 lb (1.3 kg) carrots, peeled and chopped
2 cups (500 mL) vegetable broth, plus more if needed
1 can (400 mL) unsweetened coconut milk
2 tsp (10 mL) peeled, minced ginger
Kosher salt and freshly ground black pepper to taste

**1.** In a small bowl, stir together the orange juice concentrate and water. Set aside.

**2.** In a large saucepan, heat the oil over medium heat. Add the onions and garlic and cook, stirring often, until lightly browned, about 10 minutes.

**3.** Add the orange juice mixture, carrots, 2 cups (500 mL) broth and the coconut milk. Increase the heat to high and bring to a boil. Reduce the heat to medium-low and simmer, covered, stirring occasionally, until the carrots are very soft, 30 to 45 minutes.

**4.** Using a handheld immersion blender in the saucepan (or in batches in a blender or food processor), purée the soup until smooth.

**5.** Return the soup to the saucepan if necessary, and stir in the ginger. Season with salt and pepper to taste. (If the soup is too thick for your liking, thin it with additional broth.) Heat through over medium heat before serving.

## » ONTARIO HARVEST KALE AND POTATO SOUP

### READERS' CHOICE

MAKES ABOUT 8 SERVINGS

8 to 12 oz (225 to 340 g) fresh Spanish chorizo sausage
¼ cup (60 mL) extra virgin olive oil
1 large yellow onion, chopped
1 lb (450 g) Yukon Gold or white potatoes, scrubbed and thinly sliced
2 large cloves garlic, minced
6 cups (1.5 L) vegetable broth or water
¼ cup (60 mL) apple juice
2 tsp (10 mL) kosher salt, plus more for seasoning
1 bunch kale, thick stems removed and leaves very finely sliced crosswise
Freshly ground black pepper to taste

"This is a hearty and tasty meal."

**JESSE FRAYNE**, TORONTO

Ontario's fall harvest of kale and potatoes inspired chef Steffan Howard of the Pegasus Hospitality Group (pegasushospitality .ca) to create this soup for the Harvest Grille at the Royal Agricultural Winter Fair in 2010. *Star* reader Jesse Frayne's verdict is short and to the point but says it all.

The soup leans heavily on a spicy kick from fresh Spanish chorizo—pork sausage with smoked paprika. I get my sausages from Segovia Meat Market in Kensington Market.

**1.** Preheat the oven to 375°F (190°C). Prick the sausages once each with a fork and put them on a baking sheet. Bake in the oven until cooked through, 20 to 25 minutes. Let the sausages cool for 5 minutes, then slice them thinly. Set aside on a plate.

**2.** Meanwhile, heat the oil in a large saucepan over medium heat. Add the onion and cook, stirring often, until softened, about 8 minutes. Add the potatoes and garlic and cook, stirring, for 2 minutes.

**3.** Add the broth or water, apple juice and 2 tsp (10 mL) salt. Increase the heat to high and bring to a boil. Reduce the heat to low and simmer, covered, stirring occasionally, until the potatoes are very soft, about 25 minutes.

**4.** Mash the potatoes to a purée with a potato masher or a wooden spoon. Add the cooked sausage with any juices that have accumulated on the plate. Cook over low heat for 5 minutes just to heat through.

**5.** Stir in the kale, in batches. Simmer, uncovered, until the kale is bright green and still slightly crunchy, 3 to 5 minutes. Taste and season with more salt and with pepper if necessary.

## » PANGAEA'S LEMON-PARSNIP SOUP

MAKES ABOUT 4 SERVINGS

1 tbsp (15 mL) unsalted butter

½ cup (125 mL) diced onion (preferably Spanish or sweet)

4 cups (1 L) vegetable broth, chicken broth or water

1 lb (450 g) parsnips, peeled and diced (about 2 cups/500 mL)

1 tbsp (15 mL) finely grated lemon zest (from 2 to 3 lemons)

Fine sea salt to taste

"Although I have clipped many recipes over the years, and make lots of soup, our current favourite is the lemon-parsnip soup. It gets rave reviews from three generations of our family."

**NANCY ROGERS,** MISSISSAUGA, ONT.

Toronto chef Martin Kouprie came up with this compelling soup for *Pangaea: Why It Tastes So Good* (Key Porter Books, 2011). He cooks with unprocessed, seasonal ingredients in his Yorkville restaurant Pangaea (pangaearestaurant.com), and I love how this soup tastes creamy without containing a drop of cream.

**1.** In a medium saucepan, melt the butter over medium heat until it foams. Add the onion and cook, stirring, for 3 minutes.

**2.** Add the broth or water and parsnips. Increase the heat to high and bring to a boil. Stir in the lemon zest. Reduce the heat to medium and simmer, uncovered, until the parsnips are tender, about 20 minutes.

**3.** Using a handheld immersion blender in the saucepan (or in batches in a blender or food processor), purée the soup until smooth.

**4.** Return the soup to the saucepan if necessary. Taste and season with salt if desired. Reheat the soup over low heat before serving.

"Everyone loves this soup. It's so tasty, healthy and easy to make and the texture is wonderful. I've served it as a starter for Christmas dinner, in my grandmother's tea-cups, and casually in bowls for lunch on a Saturday."

**NANCY WALLACE,** TORONTO

I travelled to Waterford in 2006 to meet Bob and Juli Proracki who grow sweet potatoes at their Round Plains Plantation. They also have a commercial kitchen where Juli whips up sweet potato treats, like this hearty soup. You can find the Prorackis at ontariosweetpotato.com and numerous Toronto farmers' markets. Juli stirred ½ cup (125 mL) evaporated milk into this soup after it was puréed, but I find it creamy-tasting enough without.

**1.** In a large saucepan, heat the oil over medium heat. Add the onion and garlic, and cook, stirring often, until softened, about 7 minutes.

**2.** Add the sweet potatoes, 3 cups (750 mL) broth or water, the cilantro, honey, curry powder and ginger. Increase the heat to high and bring to a boil. Reduce the heat to medium-low and simmer, covered, until the sweet potatoes are very tender, 30 to 40 minutes.

**3.** Using a handheld immersion blender in the saucepan (or in batches in a blender or food processor), purée the soup until smooth.

**4.** Return the soup to the saucepan if necessary. (If the soup is too thick for your liking, thin it with additional broth.) Heat through over medium heat before serving.

# CURRIED ONTARIO SWEET POTATO SOUP

Ⓡ Ⓔ Ⓐ Ⓓ Ⓔ Ⓡ Ⓢ '
Ⓒ Ⓗ Ⓞ Ⓘ Ⓒ Ⓔ

MAKES ABOUT 4 SERVINGS

1 tbsp (15 mL) vegetable oil

1 cup (250 mL) finely chopped red onion

1 large clove garlic, minced

2 lb (900 g) sweet potatoes, peeled and chopped

3 cups (750 mL) vegetable broth or water, plus more if needed

1 tbsp (15 mL) chopped cilantro

1 tsp (5 mL) liquid honey

½ tsp (2 mL) curry powder

½ tsp (2 mL) ground ginger

## » MISO SOUP WITH ENOKI MUSHROOMS

MAKES ABOUT 4 SERVINGS

4 cups (1 L) water
2 tsp (10 mL) hon dashi granules
  (bonito soup stock)
¼ cup (60 mL) shiro (white)
  miso paste
8 oz (225 g) enoki mushrooms,
  trimmed and halved
8 oz (225 g) soft or regular tofu,
  cut into small cubes
2 green onions, very thinly
  sliced

While researching a 2010 story about the dearth of female sushi chefs in the city, I was invited to the Japanese consul-general's home. His chef, Mina Makimine, created an exquisite, multi-course lunch that included this soup.

Of course, Mina (who's now back in Japan) made dashi broth from scratch with kombu (dried kelp), katsuobushi (dried bonito/tuna flakes) and niboshi (dried baby sardines/anchovies), but I prefer the ease of buying hon dashi granules from the closest Asian supermarket. Enoki mushrooms, with their long, thin stems and tiny button caps, are very delicate and often eaten raw.

**1.** In a medium saucepan, bring the water and dashi granules to a boil over high heat. Reduce the heat to medium-high.

**2.** Set a fine-mesh sieve over the saucepan and put the miso in the sieve. Using a balloon whisk, press the miso through the sieve into the broth. Alternatively, ladle ½ cup (125 mL) of the broth from the saucepan into a small bowl. Whisk the miso into the broth in the bowl, then add it back to the broth in the saucepan, whisking well.

**3.** Add the mushrooms and tofu to the broth and bring to a boil. Cook for 1 minute to heat through. Ladle into 4 bowls and scatter the green onions evenly over each portion.

Anita Stewart (anitastewart.ca) is a culinary activist and cookbook author who explores Canadian cuisine and has been made a member of the Order of Canada for her work. Anita served me this soup in her home in Elora and I have made it for just about everybody I know. It was created by the late Nettie Stanoyev, a Yugoslavian widow living in Saskatchewan who became a step-grandmother to Anita's friend Candice Stanoyev.

**1.** In a large pot, heat the oil over medium-high heat. Add the onion and cook, stirring often, until softened, about 5 minutes. Add the garlic and cook, stirring, for 2 minutes. Add the beans and cook, stirring, for 1 minute.

**2.** Add the diced tomatoes, with their juices, the tomato juice, dill, sugar, basil and pepper. Increase the heat to high and bring to a boil. Reduce the heat to low and simmer, uncovered, for 30 minutes so the flavours can blend. Taste and season with salt if necessary.

**3.** Serve hot, at room temperature or chilled, garnished with generous dollops of sour cream.

# GREEN AND YELLOW BEAN SOUP WITH DILL

MAKES ABOUT 6 SERVINGS

2 tbsp (30 mL) vegetable oil
1 medium yellow onion, finely diced
1 large clove garlic, minced
1 lb (450 g) mixed green and yellow beans, trimmed and cut into 1-inch (2.5 cm) pieces
1 can (28 oz/796 mL) diced tomatoes
3 cups (750 mL) canned tomato juice
½ cup (125 mL) chopped dill
1 tbsp (15 mL) granulated sugar
1 tsp (5 mL) dried basil
1 tsp (5 mL) freshly ground black pepper
Kosher salt to taste
Sour cream for serving

## » TIBETAN VEGETABLE SOUP WITH HAND-PULLED NOODLES

MAKES ABOUT 6 SERVINGS

2 cups (500 mL) Hand-Pulled
    Noodles (recipe on p 81)
3 tbsp (45 mL) vegetable oil
1 large yellow onion, finely diced
2 tbsp (30 mL) finely chopped,
    peeled ginger
3 cloves garlic, minced
1 tomato, diced
8 cups (2 L) water
1 medium daikon radish (about
    1-½ lb/680 g), peeled, cut
    into thin rounds, then
    julienned (about 4 cups/1 L)
2 tbsp (30 mL) soy sauce
6 oz (170 g) spinach, trimmed
    and leaves and stems
    chopped (about 8 cups/2 L)
Kosher salt to taste
Hot sauce (optional)

Nawang Galing, a Tibetan senior, cooked this soup (called *thenthuk* in Tibet) for the Dalai Lama, and he recreated it for me in his Toronto home. Nawang favours "loose spinach" from Chinatown that has thin, flat leaves and is sold whole with its roots attached, but you can use any variety.

**1.** Prepare the Hand-Pulled Noodles (recipe follows), then set aside while you make the soup.

**2.** In a large pot, heat the oil over medium-high heat. Add the onion, ginger and garlic, and cook, stirring often, until the onion is softened, about 5 minutes.

**3.** Add the tomato and cook, stirring, for 1 minute. Add the water, daikon radish and soy sauce, and bring to a boil.

**4.** When the soup is boiling, pick up 1 noodle and wrap it loosely around your hand. Break off 1-inch (2.5 cm) roughly shaped, flat pieces and throw them into the pot. Repeat with the remaining noodles. Once all the pieces are in the pot, stir the soup gently.

**5.** Add the spinach and cook, stirring, for 2 minutes until the noodles are cooked through and tender, and the spinach wilts. Taste and add salt if necessary. Ladle into bowls and serve with hot sauce, if desired.

Making noodles may seem daunting, but these rustic Tibetan noodles are a great place to experiment. They don't need to be pretty or perfect, and they're a delicious addition to soup.

# HAND-PULLED NOODLES

MAKES ABOUT 2 CUPS (500 ML)

1-½ cups (375 mL) all-purpose
   flour
1 large egg
½ to ¾ cup (125 mL to 185 mL)
   cold water
Vegetable oil for greasing

**1.** Put the flour in a medium bowl and make a well in it with your fingers. Break the egg into a small bowl, then tip it into the well in the flour and gently mix the ingredients together with your hand. Add ½ cup (125 mL) water and mix with your hand until the dough comes together, adding some or all of the remaining ¼ cup (60 mL) water if necessary.

**2.** Turn out the dough onto a lightly floured surface and knead until it is smooth and elastic, 2 to 3 minutes.

**3.** Pull or stretch the dough into an 18- x 2-inch (46 x 5 cm) cylinder, then cut crosswise into 6 pieces. With floured hands, roll each piece into a 4- x 1-inch (10 x 2.5 cm) cylinder.

**4.** Grease your hands with the oil and use your palms to lightly grease each piece of dough. Cover the dough loosely with plastic wrap and let stand at room temperature for 30 minutes.

**5.** Flatten each piece of dough by pinching it into a flat strip about 20 inches (50 cm) long between your thumb and fingers. Lay the noodles out in a single layer on the counter until you're ready to use them.

## » COCONUT AND CURRY CORN CHOWDER WITH CHICKEN

MAKES ABOUT 4 SERVINGS

3 tbsp (45 mL) extra virgin green olive oil
1 red bell pepper, seeded and diced
5 green onions, thinly sliced
2 tbsp (30 mL) peeled, minced ginger
1 tbsp (15 mL) minced garlic
1 tbsp (15 mL) seeded and minced jalapeño pepper or red chili
2 tsp (10 mL) curry powder
2 cups (500 mL) fresh or frozen and thawed corn kernels
1 can (400 mL) unsweetened coconut milk
1-½ cups (375 mL) chicken broth
1 tbsp (15 mL) Asian fish sauce (optional)
1 tbsp (15 mL) Thai sweet chili sauce
1 cup (250 mL) diced cooked chicken (white or dark meat)
1 cup (250 mL) cooked white or brown rice (any kind)
Juice of 1 lime
Kosher salt and freshly ground black pepper to taste
Thinly sliced basil leaves (optional)
Chopped cilantro (optional)

Paul Finkelstein is the chef/teacher behind the Screaming Avocado, a student-run classroom/café at Northwestern Secondary School in Stratford. He teaches culture and diversity through food, and his students made this chowder when I visited in 2009. Save this recipe for the holidays—it's a great way to use up leftover turkey in place of the chicken.

**1.** In a large saucepan, heat the oil over medium heat. Add the bell pepper, green onions, ginger, garlic and jalapeño pepper or red chili, and cook, stirring often, until softened, about 7 minutes. Add the curry powder and cook, stirring often, for 2 minutes.

**2.** Add the corn, coconut milk, broth, fish sauce (if using) and chili sauce. Increase the heat to high and bring to a boil. Reduce the heat to low and simmer, uncovered, for 5 minutes.

**3.** Add the chicken, rice and lime juice, and simmer just until the chicken is heated through, 3 to 5 minutes. Taste and season with salt and pepper if necessary. Ladle into bowls and serve garnished with basil and/or cilantro (if using).

During a working road trip to the Lake Erie beach town of Port Dover in 2001, I begged this chowder recipe from Sandy Muth, who was then chef of Fisherman's Catch Bar & Restaurant. Chowder is one of the few exceptions to my rule about avoiding cream while cooking.

# LAKE ERIE SMOKY CHOWDER

《

MAKES ABOUT 4 SERVINGS

1-½ lb (680 g) skin-on perch or pickerel fillets, cut into 2-inch (5 cm) pieces
Kosher salt and freshly ground black pepper to taste
1 tbsp (15 mL) vegetable oil
8 slices double-smoked bacon, chopped
24 sprigs thyme
12 mini potatoes, quartered
2 ears corn, each cut into 6 pieces or 1 cup (250 mL) fresh or frozen and thawed corn kernels
1 large zucchini, cut into ¾-inch (2 cm) rounds
4 green onions, cut into 2-inch (5 cm) pieces
4 cloves garlic, thinly sliced
2 cups (500 mL) white wine, such as Chardonnay
1-½ cups (375 mL) whipping cream
8 oz (225 g) smoked fish (such as trout or whitefish), flaked or torn into pieces
½ cup (125 mL) fresh lemon juice

**1.** Season the perch or pickerel with salt and pepper. In a large non-stick skillet, heat the oil over medium heat. Add the perch or pickerel, flesh side down, and cook until browned, about 5 minutes (fish will only be partially cooked).

**2.** Meanwhile, in a large pot over medium heat, cook the bacon and thyme, stirring often, until the bacon renders some of its fat, about 5 minutes.

**3.** Add the potatoes, corn, zucchini, green onions and garlic to the pot, and cook, stirring often, for 5 minutes.

**4.** Add the wine, cream, smoked fish and lemon juice and bring to a simmer. Cook, covered, until the potatoes are almost tender, 10 to 15 minutes.

**5.** Add the reserved fresh fish. Bring back to a simmer and cook, covered, until the fish just flakes with a fork and the chowder is heated through, 3 to 5 minutes. Taste and season with salt and pepper if necessary. Discard thyme sprigs before serving.

Maria Nanavati, who owned El Camino restaurant, showed me how to make this Mexican soup (pronounced poh-SO-leh) in 2002. Hominy is dry white or yellow corn that's soaked and cooked in an alkaline solution to remove the hull and germ. It's sold dried, but it's easier to buy it canned (see My Favourite Places to Shop, page 228). Pozole is all about the garnishes, so don't skimp.

For a variation on this recipe, try Pozole Rojo (red pozole): rinse, stem and seed 4 dried ancho chilies. Soak in a bowl with hot water to cover for 20 minutes, then purée in a mini food processor. Rub the purée through a fine-mesh sieve into the pot while the pork is cooking, discarding any solids in the sieve.

**1.** For the pozole, combine 1 cup (250 mL) water, the yellow onion, garlic, crumbled bouillon cubes and coriander seeds in a mini food processor or blender. Blend for 1 minute, then transfer to a large pot.

**2.** Add the remaining 8 cups (2 L) water, the pork and bay leaves. Bring to a boil over high heat. Reduce the heat to medium and simmer, covered, stirring occasionally and turning the pork with tongs, until the pork pulls apart easily with a fork, about 90 minutes.

**3.** Transfer the pork to a cutting board and let cool slightly. Shred the meat by hand, discarding the fat and any bone.

**4.** Discard the bay leaves from the pot. If necessary, add more water to make 8 cups (2 L) broth. Add the hominy and pork to the pot. Cook over high heat, stirring often, until heated through, 5 to 7 minutes.

**5.** For the garnishes, arrange the cabbage or lettuce, avocado, cilantro, radishes, white onion and lime wedges on a platter. Spoon the oregano and chili powder into 2 small bowls.

**6.** Ladle the soup into soup bowls and serve with the garnishes so everyone can add the garnish of their choice, rubbing the oregano between their fingers before crumbling it into the soup.

# POZOLE &raquo;

## (MEXICAN PORK AND HOMINY SOUP)

MAKES ABOUT 6 SERVINGS

**Pozole**

9 cups (2.25 L) water, plus more if needed
1 medium yellow onion, quartered
6 cloves garlic, peeled and smashed
4 chicken bouillon cubes, crumbled
1 tbsp (15 mL) coriander seeds
2-½ lb (1.1 kg) pork shoulder (butt/blade end), fat trimmed
5 bay leaves
1 can (29 oz/822 g) white hominy, drained and rinsed

**Garnishes**

Shredded green cabbage or iceberg lettuce
Peeled, pitted and sliced or chopped avocado
Chopped cilantro
Thinly sliced radishes
Minced white onion
Lime wedges
Dried oregano leaves (preferably Mexican)
Pure chili powder (such as pequín or ancho) or cayenne

# SALADS

Good for the body and soul, salads are something that we should all eat more of.

## » MASHU MASHU'S HOUSE SALAD

MAKES 2 SERVINGS

**Basil Vinaigrette**

1 cup (250 mL) tightly packed
    basil leaves
2 cloves garlic, peeled
¼ tsp (1 mL) kosher salt
¼ tsp (1 mL) freshly ground
    black pepper
⅓ cup (80 mL) extra virgin olive
    oil
2 tbsp (30 mL) balsamic vinegar
1 tbsp (15 mL) liquid honey

**Salad**

8 oz (225 g) mixed salad greens
12 grape or cherry tomatoes
2 bottled roasted red peppers,
    rinsed, patted dry and thinly
    sliced
¼ cup (60 mL) pine nuts,
    toasted
2 oz (60 g) chèvre (soft
    unripened goat cheese),
    crumbled (about ¼ cup/
    60 mL)

*Star* restaurant critic Amy Pataki calls Mashu Mashu Mediterranean Grill's house salad "a thing of wonder" and got the recipe in 2007. It's still a hit at the Forest Hill Village restaurant (mashumashu.ca), now owned by Enri Rexhmataj. Toast the pine nuts in a small, dry skillet over medium heat.

1. For the Basil Vinaigrette, combine the basil, garlic, salt and pepper in a blender or a food processor, then blend until finely minced. With the machine running, slowly pour in the oil, vinegar and honey, processing until the dressing is emulsified.

2. For the salad, toss the greens with the tomatoes, red peppers and pine nuts in a large bowl. Add half of the Basil Vinaigrette (or to taste) and toss again. Refrigerate any remaining vinaigrette in an airtight container for up to 5 days.

3. Divide the salad between 2 plates and sprinkle each portion evenly with cheese.

For those who want to avoid the anchovies, eggs or cheese in a traditional Caesar salad, this creamy, tangy, vegan version is for you. I discovered it in 2009 at the Good Food Café run by FoodShare Toronto (foodshare.net), a non-profit group that tackles hunger and food issues. It was created by natural foods chef/registered holistic nutritionist Katie Compton, of Kate and the Kitchen (kateandthekitchen.com). The recipe is now in *Share: Delicious Dishes from FoodShare and Friends* (Between the Lines, 2012) by Adrienne De Francesco with Marion Kane.

Look for vegan (anchovy-free) Worcestershire sauce in health food stores and the natural food area of most large supermarkets.

**1.** In a blender or mini food processor, combine the tofu, oil, lemon juice, garlic, vinegar, miso, Dijon, Worcestershire sauce, salt and pepper. Process until smooth, about 1 minute. Transfer to an airtight container and refrigerate until ready to use, or for up to 5 days.

**2.** In a large salad bowl, combine the romaine and ½ cup (125 mL) dressing, then toss well. Taste and add more dressing, if desired.

# FOODSHARE'S VEGAN CAESAR SALAD

MAKES 4–6 SERVINGS

¾ cup (185 mL) crumbled
    regular or medium tofu
¼ cup (60 mL) extra virgin olive
    oil
Juice of 1 lemon
1 tbsp (15 mL) minced garlic
1 tbsp (15 mL) red wine vinegar
1 tbsp (15 mL) white (shiro)
    miso paste
1 tsp (5 mL) Dijon mustard
1 tsp (5 mL) vegan
    Worcestershire sauce
½ tsp (2 mL) kosher salt
¼ tsp (1 mL) freshly ground
    black pepper
1 large head romaine,
    trimmed and chopped
    (about 12 cups/3 L)

## » CRAWFORD STREET SALAD

MAKES 4 SERVINGS

¼ cup (60 mL) fresh lemon juice

3 tbsp (45 mL) extra virgin olive oil

1 tbsp (15 mL) fresh lime juice

1 tsp (5 mL) kosher salt

Freshly ground black pepper to taste

1 cup (250 mL) chopped white onion

½ cup (125 mL) chopped cilantro

1 head green leaf lettuce, chopped or torn into bite-size pieces

1 cup (250 mL) small broccoli florets

2 plum (roma) tomatoes, halved and thickly sliced

1 avocado, peeled, pitted and chopped

My friend Adrienne Amato performs regular salad magic at her home on Crawford Street. This creation, with its salty, lemon-lime–soaked onions, is loved by all who drop by for dinner. It's inspired by the Chilean salad that we both crave from Jumbo Empanadas, a restaurant in Kensington Market.

**1.** In a medium bowl, whisk together the lemon juice, oil, lime juice and salt. Season with pepper to taste and whisk again.

**2.** Add the onion and cilantro to the lemon juice mixture and stir well, making sure the onions are covered by the liquid. Let stand for at least 15 minutes or refrigerate, covered, for several hours.

**3.** Put the lettuce in a large salad bowl and top with the broccoli, tomatoes and avocado.

**4.** Just before serving, pour the onion mixture over the lettuce mixture and toss well.

## » JAPANESE HOUSE SALAD WITH GINGER DRESSING

MAKES 4 SERVINGS

### Ginger Dressing

¾ cup (185 mL) canola or
 vegetable oil
1 small yellow onion, chopped
3 tbsp (45 mL) unseasoned rice
 vinegar
3 tbsp (45 mL) soy sauce
1-inch (2.5 cm) piece ginger,
 peeled and chopped
1 tbsp (15 mL) beaten egg
 (optional)

### Salad

4 cups (1 L) chopped iceberg,
 romaine and/or mixed baby
 greens
1 cup (250 mL) peeled and
 julienned or shredded carrots

One of my favourite things at cheap sushi restaurants is the house salad (usually just iceberg lettuce and shredded carrots) with ginger dressing. No two dressings taste the same, though they're all variations on the same theme.

Freelance writer Cynthia David (cynthia-david.com) found the first incarnation of this dressing recipe in 2004 at Taki Japanese Restaurant (niagaratakirestaurant.com) in Niagara Falls. Chef/owner Tomo Izumita has tweaked the recipe and now adds a raw egg to make it rich and creamy. If that's a health concern for you, just leave it out.

**1.** For the Ginger Dressing, combine the oil, onion, vinegar, soy sauce, ginger and egg (if using) in a blender or food processor. Process until smooth, about 1 minute. Transfer to an airtight container and refrigerate until ready to use, or for up to 5 days. Shake well before using.

**2.** For the salad, divide the lettuce and/or baby greens among 4 plates or bowls. Top each with a pile of carrot, then drizzle each salad with Ginger Dressing to taste, reserving the remaining dressing for another use.

Galleria Supermarket (galleriasm.com), with branches in Thornhill and Don Mills, is my top destination for Korean groceries. I learned to make this salad from Jinah Choi, the supermarket's head chef, during a public cooking demo. While most kimchi (pickled vegetables) takes ages to ferment, this version can be made in less than an hour.

**1.** For the salad, put the cabbage in a large bowl. In a measuring cup, stir together the water and salt, then pour over the cabbage, mixing it with your hands. Let the cabbage stand, mixing it occasionally, until the strips bend without snapping, about 30 minutes. Rinse twice and drain well.

**2.** Chop the cabbage into 3-inch (7.5 cm) lengths and put it in a large salad bowl, along with the pear, apple and green onions.

**3.** For the dressing, stir together the water and flour in a small saucepan over medium heat. Cook, whisking constantly, until a thick and glue-like paste forms, 3 to 5 minutes. Remove the saucepan from the heat.

**4.** Spoon 1 tbsp (15 mL) of the paste into a medium bowl, discarding the remaining paste or reserving it for another use.

**5.** Add the red pepper powder, fish or anchovy sauce, apple or ginger ale, honey, garlic, ginger and sugar to the flour paste, and whisk well.

**6.** Pour half of the dressing over the cabbage mixture, then toss well. If desired, add some or all of the remaining dressing, tossing again until well combined. Sprinkle with sesame seeds (if using).

# KIMCHI AND ASIAN PEAR SALAD

«

MAKES 4–6 SERVINGS

**Salad**

¼ napa cabbage, cored and thinly sliced lengthwise into long strips

2 cups (500 mL) cold water

2 tbsp (30 mL) coarse sea or kosher salt

½ Asian (Korean) pear, peeled, cored and julienned

½ Fuji or other sweet, crisp apple, peeled, cored and julienned

2 green onions, cut into long thin strips

**Dressing**

⅓ cup (80 mL) water

1 tsp (5 mL) all-purpose or sweet rice flour

3 tbsp (45 mL) Korean coarse red pepper powder

1-½ tbsp (22 mL) Asian fish sauce or Korean anchovy sauce

1 tbsp (15 mL) puréed peeled apple or ginger ale

1 tbsp (15 mL) liquid honey

2 tsp (10 mL) minced garlic

1 tsp (5 mL) peeled, minced ginger

½ tsp (2 mL) granulated sugar

Toasted sesame seeds (optional)

"Tried it and made it for a couple of potluck suppers. Every single solitary person wanted the recipe. So easy, so light and so unusual to have a salad that uses watermelon as an ingredient. It is now part of my permanent repertoire."

**NINA CAMERON,** PORT ROWAN, ONT.

Sweet, juicy watermelon stars in this very adult salad that's rounded out by salty feta and fragrant basil and olive oil. Watermelon salads exploded onto the Toronto restaurant scene in 2011 and I featured three cross-cultural recipes in a story called "Watermelon grows up."

This version, the simplest of the trio, was inspired by Yotam Ottolenghi (ottolenghi.co.uk), who has a chain of takeout stores and a restaurant in London, UK, and a recipe from his book *Plenty: Vibrant Vegetable Recipes from London's Ottolenghi* (Chronicle Books, 2011). Some variations to consider are mint, cilantro or parsley instead of basil, the addition of tomatoes or oranges, and adding a splash of balsamic vinegar or fresh lemon juice.

**1.** On a serving platter, loosely scatter the watermelon, feta, basil and onion. Drizzle with oil to taste.

# WATERMELON AND FETA SALAD

MAKES 4–6 SERVINGS

4 cups (1 L) bite-size (about 1-inch/2.5 cm) chunks watermelon

6 oz (175 g) feta, broken into small chunks or chopped

1 bunch basil, stems discarded and large leaves chopped but small leaves left whole

1 small red onion, halved and very thinly sliced

Fruity extra virgin olive oil to taste

## » KALE AND ARUGULA SALAD

### READERS' CHOICE

MAKES 4 SERVINGS

**Cayenne-White Balsamic Dressing**

3 tbsp (45 mL) extra virgin olive oil

2 tbsp (30 mL) white balsamic vinegar

1 tsp (5 mL) cayenne

1 tsp (5 mL) freshly ground black pepper

1 tsp (5 mL) Herbamare (herbed salt)

1 tsp (5 mL) fresh lemon juice

**Garlic Chips (optional)**

¼ cup (60 mL) coconut or vegetable oil

¼ cup (60 mL) very thinly sliced garlic cloves

**Salad**

4 cups (1 L) packed chopped kale leaves

2 cups (500 mL) baby arugula, chopped if desired

16 cherry or grape tomatoes (or a combination), halved

½ cup (125 mL) chopped green onions (about 5)

"Both kale and arugula are nutritional powerhouses. I love the texture and it feels that you are eating a meal, something with substance, and not just a watery salad. The freshly made garlic chips elevate this salad to a higher plateau."

**KAY VAN-LANE,** MISSISSAUGA, ONT.

The Gourmet Bitches (gourmetb1tches.com) is a gluten-free, health-minded food truck run by Bianka Matchett and Shontelle Pinch, and this is one of their signature dishes. It's lovely to see raw kale used in a salad for a change, and the assertive dressing stands up to the dark, leafy green.

Herbamare, sold in spice shakers in supermarkets and health food stores, is a mix of natural sea salt marinated with dried herbs and vegetables. It's easy to make the garlic chips, but you can buy bags of fried garlic in Asian supermarkets, too (you'll need ¼ cup/ 60 mL for the salad). Dial down the cayenne in the dressing if you like less spice.

**1.** For the Cayenne-White Balsamic Dressing, whisk together the oil, vinegar, cayenne, black pepper, Herbamare and lemon juice in a small bowl. Set aside.

**2.** For the Garlic Chips, heat the oil in a small skillet over medium heat. Add the garlic and cook, stirring often, until golden, 4 to 5 minutes. Remove the garlic with a slotted spoon and let drain on paper towels. Refrigerate in an airtight container for up to 1 day.

**3.** For the salad, toss together the kale and arugula in a large bowl. Add the dressing to taste and toss well. Add the tomatoes, green onions and Garlic Chips (if using), and toss again. Divide the salad among 4 plates. Alternatively, divide the dressed kale and arugula among 4 plates and let people garnish their own salad with the tomatoes, onions and Garlic Chips.

I love freelance writer Eric Vellend's bright, modern, tangy coleslaw—no mayo required.

**1.** For the slaw, toss together the onion and vinegar in a large salad bowl and let stand for 10 minutes. Add the cabbage, carrot, cilantro and chili, and toss well.

**2.** For the vinaigrette, whisk together the sugar and Dijon in a small bowl. Slowly whisk in the vinegar followed by the oil until the vinaigrette is smooth and slightly thickened. Season with salt and pepper to taste.

**3.** Just before serving, whisk the vinaigrette, pour it over the slaw and toss well.

# MODERN SLAW WITH VINAIGRETTE

MAKES 6–8 SERVINGS

**Slaw**
¼ cup (60 mL) thinly sliced red
    onion (in half moons)
2 tsp (10 mL) red wine vinegar
1 lb (450 g) green cabbage, outer
    leaves and core discarded,
    and very thinly sliced or
    shredded in a food processor
1 carrot, peeled and julienned
⅓ cup (80 mL) chopped
    cilantro
1 fresh red chili (about
    5 inches/12.5 cm), seeded,
    if desired, and minced

**Vinaigrette**
2 tsp (10 mL) granulated sugar
2 tsp (10 mL) Dijon mustard
¼ cup (60 mL) cider vinegar
3 tbsp (45 mL) vegetable oil
Kosher salt and freshly ground
    black pepper to taste

## » ONTARIO BUFFALO MOZZARELLA WITH TOMATOES AND BASIL

### ⓇⒺⒶⒹⒺⓇⓈ' ⒸⒽⓄⒾⒸⒺ

MAKES 4–6 SERVINGS

1 container (12 oz/340 g) grape
    tomatoes
Extra virgin olive oil to taste
Fine sea salt to taste
1 container (180 g) mini buffalo
    mozzarella balls (about 18),
    torn in half
Chopped or shredded leaves
    from 1 bunch basil
Flaky sea salt and freshly ground
    black pepper to taste

"I used to serve this salad on a platter as suggested in the recipe but found that some, previously very well-behaved, dinner guests became quite aggressive in taking a larger than normal portion for themselves. So I now portion out the salad myself. But it doesn't seem to stop them stealing from each other's plates! All in good fun, mind you."

**JOANNA MACKINNON,** TORONTO

Meeting the water buffalo at Martin Littkemann and Lori Smith's farm near Stirling, Ontario, in 2010 was a good day's work. The couple runs the Ontario Water Buffalo Co. and sells milk to Quality Cheese (qualitycheese.com) in Vaughan from which Ontario buffalo mozzarella is made.

Quality Cheese created this caprese salad and, because the tomatoes are roasted, it tastes good even when Ontario tomatoes aren't in season. The company's Bella Casara buffalo mozzarella is sold in many supermarkets. I prefer the mini balls, but you could buy the 125-gram tub that contains one large ball, and tear it into chunks.

**1.** Preheat the oven to 200°F (100°C). On a rimmed baking sheet, spread out the tomatoes in a single layer. Drizzle them lightly with oil and sprinkle with fine sea salt.

**2.** Bake in the oven until the tomatoes are wrinkled and tender, 3 to 4 hours. Remove from the oven and let cool to room temperature.

**3.** On a serving platter, scatter the tomatoes and buffalo mozzarella. Sprinkle with basil and drizzle with oil. Season to taste with flaky sea salt and pepper. For best flavour, let stand at room temperature for 30 to 60 minutes before serving.

I fell in love with nutritious and delicious quinoa ("keen-wah"), the nutty, grain-like seed, long before it leapt from health food stores into the mainstream. FoodShare Toronto (foodshare.net), a non-profit community group that tackles hunger and food issues, served this at a salad bar fundraiser in 2004.

Look for Hempola brand (from Barrie, Ont.) or Manitoba Harvest (from Winnipeg) shelled hemp seeds and hemp oil in the refrigerated sections of health food stores and the natural food sections of some large supermarkets.

**1.** For the salad, bring the water to a boil in a small saucepan over high heat. Add the quinoa. Reduce the heat to low and simmer, covered, until the water has been absorbed, about 12 minutes. Remove the saucepan from the heat and let stand for 5 minutes. Fluff the quinoa with a fork.

**2.** In a large salad bowl, stir together the quinoa, carrot, bell pepper, hemp seeds, parsley, cranberries and pumpkin seeds.

**3.** For the dressing, whisk together the oil, lemon juice, soy sauce and honey in a small bowl. Season with salt and pepper to taste and whisk again.

**4.** Pour the dressing over the quinoa mixture and toss well. Let stand at room temperature for at least 30 minutes to let the flavours develop.

# CRANBERRY, HEMP AND QUINOA SALAD

MAKES 4–6 SERVINGS

**Salad**
2 cups (500 mL) water
1 cup (250 mL) dried quinoa, rinsed
1 large carrot, peeled and grated
1 red bell pepper, seeded and chopped
½ cup (125 mL) shelled hemp seeds
½ cup (125 mL) chopped flat-leaf parsley
¼ cup (60 mL) dried cranberries
¼ cup (60 mL) raw green shelled pumpkin seeds (pepitas)

**Dressing**
2 tbsp (30 mL) hemp oil
2 tbsp (30 mL) fresh lemon juice
1 tsp (5 mL) soy sauce
½ tsp (2 mL) liquid honey
Kosher salt and freshly ground black pepper to taste

*Left: Raw green shelled pumpkin seeds (pepitas)*

## » TOMATO AND CILANTRO SALAD

MAKES 4 SERVINGS

5 tomatoes, quartered and thinly
  sliced
1 cup (250 mL) chopped
  cilantro
3 tbsp (45 mL) extra virgin olive
  oil
2 tbsp (30 mL) fresh lemon juice
1 tbsp (15 mL) white vinegar
1 clove garlic, minced
1 tsp (5 mL) kosher salt
½ tsp (2 mL) freshly ground
  black pepper
Pinch cayenne

While North American salads usually revolve around lettuce and bottled dressings, Arab salads celebrate fresh herbs, spices, grains, pulses and more. Habeeb Salloum, a Toronto cookbook author and Middle Eastern food expert, gave us this one from Yemen in a 2004 salad story headlined "So fresh and so green." For best flavour, never refrigerate tomatoes.

**1.** In a medium salad bowl, gently toss together the tomatoes and cilantro.

**2.** In a small bowl, whisk together the oil, lemon juice, vinegar, garlic, salt, black pepper and cayenne.

**3.** Just before serving, pour the dressing over the tomato mixture and toss gently.

"This salad is amazing and delicious and so easy to make. We eat it for lunch or dinner as a side dish. Company loves when we have served it and I have given the recipe to many friends. It's healthy and just so easy to put together."

**LINDA COLLINS,** HAMILTON, ONT.

For my *What's for Dinner* series I go into people's homes and see what they really eat on a weeknight. Debbie Cheng, a Toronto educator, makes this salad on the weekend to take for work lunches or to build on for weeknight dinners. Chop your onion, pepper and broccoli so they're no larger than the kidney beans. When I was over, Debbie ate this with baked salmon and a cold quinoa-edamame salad.

**1.** In a medium salad bowl, combine the chickpeas, kidney beans, onion, bell pepper and broccoli.

**2.** In a small bowl, whisk together the vinegar, oil, Dijon, honey, paprika, cumin and salt.

**3.** Pour the dressing over the chickpea mixture and toss well. Refrigerate, tightly covered, for at least 2 hours to let the flavours develop.

# DEBBIE CHENG'S TWO-BEAN SALAD

«

READERS' CHOICE

MAKES 6–8 SERVINGS

1 can (19 oz/540 mL) chickpeas, drained and rinsed
1 can (19 oz/540 mL) red kidney beans, drained and rinsed
½ medium red onion, diced (about ½ cup/125 mL)
½ red bell pepper, seeded and diced
Handful broccoli florets, chopped very small
¼ cup (60 mL) red wine vinegar
2 tbsp (30 mL) extra virgin olive oil
2 tbsp (30 mL) Dijon mustard
2 tbsp (30 mL) liquid honey
1 tbsp (15 mL) paprika
Pinch ground cumin
Pinch fine sea salt

# MEAT, CHICKEN AND FISH MAINS

My husband is a bison rancher, so when I'm eating meat for pleasure, it's usually ours. But in the line of duty, I eat everything. I also love Ontario lake fish, but am always keen to see what else my fishmonger has.

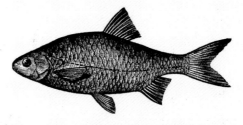

*Left: Pancetta and guanciale*

*What's for Dinner*, where I go into people's homes and watch them make a weekday dinner, is a regular feature in the *Star*'s food section. At the apartment shared by 20-somethings Eli Curi and Shehzad Hamza, the men (a computer systems analyst and a marketing analyst, respectively) cooked both Lebanese-Mexican and Indian food. Eli's background is Mexican, Lebanese, Spanish and French, and this is his creation which he eats with rice and sliced cucumbers dressed with yogurt, cilantro and mint.

**1.** For the kaftas, combine the beef, mint, onion and parsley in a medium bowl. Season with pepper to taste. Mix well with your hands, massaging the seasonings into the meat.

**2.** Divide the beef mixture into 8 even-size pieces and shape each into a fat oval or cigar-shaped patty (kafta), about 3 x 1 inches (7.5 x 2.5 cm). Refrigerate, covered, for at least 1 hour.

**3.** Heat a large cast iron or regular skillet over medium-high heat. Add the oil, then the kaftas. Cook, turning often, until they are browned on all sides and no longer pink inside, about 10 minutes. Transfer the kaftas to a serving plate and keep warm.

**4.** For the Tahini-Lime Sauce, whisk together the tahini, ¼ cup (60 mL) water and lime juice in a small bowl until smooth. If needed, add a little more water, 1 tbsp (15 mL) at a time, until the sauce is a pourable consistency. Serve the kaftas with the sauce.

# BEEF KAFTAS WITH TAHINI-LIME SAUCE ≪

MAKES 8

### Kaftas
1 lb (450 g) ground beef
½ cup (125 mL) mint leaves, chopped
¼ cup (60 mL) finely diced white onion
¼ cup (60 mL) flat-leaf parsley leaves, chopped
Freshly ground black pepper to taste
1 tbsp (15 mL) vegetable oil

### Tahini-Lime Sauce
¼ cup (60 mL) well-stirred tahini (sesame paste)
¼ cup (60 mL) water, or more as needed
Juice of 1 lime

## » AFGHAN CHAPLEE KABOBS

MAKES 6

1-½ tbsp (22 mL) coriander
    seeds
2 cloves garlic, smashed
1 jalapeño pepper or fresh green
    chili, stem removed
1 medium yellow onion,
    chopped
1 lb (450 g) medium ground beef
1 tbsp (15 mL) dried red chili
    flakes
1 tsp (5 mL) kosher salt
1 tbsp (15 mL) vegetable oil
Ground sumac for sprinkling
    (optional)

These zingy kabobs are really just bunless burgers which, in Afghan restaurants, are served with basmati rice, salad and flatbread. Haroon and Jameel Amadi, brothers who own Kabob Express (kabobexpress.ca) in Vaughan, shared this recipe with me.

Ground sumac is the dried, ground berry of a shrub that grows in the Middle East, and gives a slightly tart flavour to the kabobs. Play around with the amounts of coriander, red chili flakes and fresh chilies and, for extra heat, use small, green bird's eye chilies.

**1.** In a small, dry skillet, toast the coriander seeds over medium-high heat until fragrant, 5 to 7 minutes. Grind the seeds in a mortar using a pestle, or pulse them until coarsely ground in a coffee grinder reserved for spices or in a mini food processor.

**2.** In a mini food processor, pulse the garlic and jalapeño or chili until minced. Add the onion and pulse just until minced. (Don't overprocess the vegetables or they'll turn to liquid.)

**3.** Transfer the garlic mixture to a medium bowl. Add the coriander seeds, beef, red chili flakes and salt and mix well by hand. Divide the beef mixture into 6 even-size balls then flatten each into a thin patty, about 4 to 5 inches (10 to 13 cm) in diameter.

**4.** Heat the oil in a large non-stick skillet over medium heat. Add enough patties to the skillet to fit without crowding and sprinkle them with a little sumac (if using). Cook until browned on the undersides. Flip the patties and sprinkle with a little more sumac (if using), then cook until browned on the outside and no longer pink inside, 3 to 5 minutes. Repeat with the remaining patties.

The smashed burger trend reached Toronto around 2010, with The Stockyards (thestockyards.ca), Burger's Priest (theburgerspriest.com) and Five Guys Burgers and Fries (fiveguys .ca) all offering up flat, crispy, juicy burgers. After getting tips from the experts, I perfected the technique at home using a cast iron skillet. A few keys: smash the burgers once with a strong (not flimsy) spatula, use pure ground meat with no filler and ask your butcher for ground beef with a meat-to-fat ratio of about 80:20.

**1.** Heat a large cast iron skillet over medium heat for 10 minutes.

**2.** Meanwhile, without overhandling the meat, loosely form it into 4 balls. Sprinkle the tops with salt (if using). Put 2 balls, salt sides down, in the hot skillet and cook, undisturbed, for 1 minute.

**3.** Using a large, heavy, unperforated metal spatula, quickly flatten each ball to a 5-inch (13 cm) patty. Brush each patty with 1 tbsp (15 mL) mustard (if using), then cook for 2-½ minutes. Carefully flip each burger, scraping up any crusty brown bits from the bottom of the skillet. (Do not press down on the burgers.)

**4.** Add 1 slice cheese to each burger (if using), then cook for 2-½ minutes until the undersides are browned and the burgers are no longer pink inside. (Cover the skillet with a lid for the final minute of cooking if the cheese isn't melting.)

**5.** Transfer the burgers to a plate, cover loosely with foil and keep warm. Repeat with the remaining burgers.

**6.** Serve the burgers in buns with your favourite burger toppings.

# SMASHED BURGERS

MAKES 4

1-¼ lb (565 g) ground beef (preferably medium or regular)
Kosher salt (optional)
4 tbsp (60 mL) yellow mustard (optional)
4 slices aged cheddar cheese (optional)
4 soft buns, sliced open and warmed or toasted, and buttered if desired
Your favourite burger toppings

## » BISON BURGERS WITH SMOKED GOUDA

MAKES 6

1 large egg
1 tbsp (15 mL) extra virgin olive oil
1-½ lb (680 g) ground bison
1 small red onion, finely diced
¼ cup (60 mL) fresh bread crumbs
¼ cup (60 mL) chopped flat-leaf parsley
1 large clove garlic, minced
1 fresh red chili (about 4 inches/ 10 cm long), seeded if desired and minced
1 tbsp (15 mL) Dijon mustard
1 tbsp (15 mL) whole grain mustard
Finely grated zest of 1 lemon
Canola oil for cooking
6 thin slices smoked Gouda
6 hamburger buns, sliced open and toasted or warmed if desired

At St. Joseph's Health Centre, head chef John Butler has turned the money-losing cafeteria into something to be proud of. When I visited in 2011, these gorgeous, restaurant-worthy burgers were a daily special for just $4.99.

Some upscale butchers sell bison. The Canadian Bison Association has a "where to buy" link at canadianbison.ca for farm-gate sales, farmers' markets and some retail. If it's hard to find, you can substitute ground beef (and smoked cheddar for the Gouda). These burgers are swoon-inducing on their own, but send them over the top with John's spicy-sweet Red Pepper Relish (page 47).

**1.** In a large bowl, whisk together the egg and olive oil. Add the bison, onion, bread crumbs, parsley, garlic, red chili, Dijon and whole grain mustards and lemon zest. Mix thoroughly with your hands, massaging the ingredients together. Divide into 6 even-size pieces and roll into balls. With your hand, flatten each ball into a ¾-inch (2 cm) thick burger, about 4 inches (10 cm) in diameter.

**2.** Lay the burgers on a baking sheet and cover with plastic wrap. Refrigerate for at least 1 hour so the patties are cold when they are cooked.

**3.** When ready to cook, heat a large, lightly oiled cast iron or non-stick skillet over medium-high heat. Cook the burgers (in batches if necessary) until they're no longer pink inside, about 5 minutes per side, reducing the heat slightly if the burgers brown too much, and topping each burger with a slice of cheese for the last minute of cooking. Serve the burgers in the buns.

Bulgogi is the marinated beef that you grill at your table in Korean restaurants. Buy the meat at Korean supermarkets (see My Favourite Places to Shop, page 228), or it won't be sliced thinly enough to be tender for this recipe and the one that follows. Jimmy Kwon and his wife, Si Sook Kim, who run Woori Meat Shop in Mississauga, invited me to visit their store in 2009, made me lunch and gave me a few family recipes, including this one.

1. In a large, resealable plastic bag, combine the sugar, soy sauce, water, pear or onion, garlic, honey or corn syrup, mirin, sesame oil and pepper. Add the meat to the bag (it will curl up), then refrigerate for at least 3 hours or up to 12 hours, turning the bag occasionally.

2. When ready to cook, heat a large non-stick wok or skillet over medium-high heat. Add the meat, with its marinade, and cook, stirring often, until the meat is cooked and the mixture is almost dry, 5 to 8 minutes.

3. To serve, set out separate bowls or plates of the meat, lettuce, sesame seeds and pepper paste.

4. To assemble, put a small amount of beef (1 large piece, or as desired) in the centre of a lettuce leaf. Sprinkle with sesame seeds, top with a small dollop of red pepper paste, then roll into a pouch.

# BULGOGI LETTUCE WRAPS　《

MAKES ABOUT 6 SERVINGS

5 tbsp (75 mL) granulated sugar
5 tbsp (75 mL) soy sauce
5 tbsp (75 mL) water
¼ cup (60 mL) peeled, cored and puréed Asian pear or yellow onion
5 large cloves garlic, minced
1 tbsp (15 mL) liquid honey or corn syrup
2 tsp (10 mL) mirin (Japanese sweet rice cooking wine)
1 tsp (5 mL) sesame oil
½ tsp (2 mL) freshly ground black pepper
About 2 lb (900 g) Korean bulgogi (very thinly sliced, boneless beef rib-eye)
1 head red leaf lettuce, leaves separated and washed and dried
Toasted sesame seeds for serving
Korean hot red pepper paste (gochujang)

Don't be put off by the length of this recipe—it's all about the optional toppings. Bibimbap ("mixed rice"), a bowl of rice with four to six toppings and hot pepper paste, is one of Korea's signature dishes. When it's served, it's beautiful to behold. When it's mixed together, it becomes a feast. This recipe comes from Patricia Wong, a writer and researcher on traditional Korean cuisine and dance. Omit the beef for a vegetarian main dish.

**1.** For the rice, combine the rice and ginger in a rice cooker. Add the water and cook according to the machine's instructions. Fluff with a fork, discarding the ginger. (Alternatively, cook the rice and ginger together following your usual method.) Keep warm.

**2.** For the beef, combine the bulgogi, pear, sugar, sesame oil and soy sauce in a medium bowl. Let stand at room temperature for at least 15 minutes or cover and refrigerate for several hours.

**3.** Heat a medium non-stick skillet over medium-high heat. Add the meat and marinade. Cook, stirring often, until the meat is cooked through and the marinade is sticky and has nearly evaporated, about 3 minutes. Remove from the heat and keep warm.

**4.** For the toppings, heat the oil in a large non-stick skillet over medium-high heat. Add the mushroom caps and cook, stirring often, until they release and reabsorb their liquid, 6 to 8 minutes. Remove the mushrooms to a small serving bowl.

**5.** Either put the raw carrots, cucumber and bean sprouts in separate bowls, or stir-fry them separately for 1 to 2 minutes first, then transfer to separate bowls. Put the seaweed in a separate bowl.

**6.** Either separate the egg, discarding the white, and put the raw yolk in a small bowl, or fry the whole egg in a lightly oiled non-stick skillet over medium-high heat, until the white is set and the yolk is still runny.

**7.** To serve the bibimbap, put the sesame seeds and sesame oil in a large serving bowl. Add the rice and pat it down. Spoon the red pepper paste in the centre of the rice, then carefully slide the raw egg yolk (if using) alongside the red pepper paste. Arrange the beef and other toppings of your choice in neat piles in the bowl, fanning them out from the red pepper paste. Put the fried egg (if using) in the centre of the bowl. At the table, toss the ingredients together and divide among 4 individual bowls.

# BIBIMBAP ≪
## (KOREAN RICE BOWL)

MAKES 4 SERVINGS

### Rice
1-½ cups (375 mL) white or
   brown medium-grain rice
4 thin slices ginger

### Beef
8 oz (225 g) Korean bulgogi
   (very thinly sliced, boneless
   beef rib-eye), julienned
¼ Asian pear, peeled, cored and
   grated
2 tsp (10 mL) light brown sugar
2 tsp (10 mL) sesame oil
2 tsp (10 mL) dark soy sauce

### Optional Toppings
1 tbsp (15 mL) vegetable oil
6 shiitake mushroom caps,
   julienned
½ cup (125 mL) peeled and
   julienned carrots
½ cup (125 mL) julienned
   English cucumber
½ cup (125 mL) bean sprouts
   (preferably mung bean),
   washed
½ cup (125 mL) thinly sliced
   roasted seaweed (laver), such
   as nori
1 large egg
1 tbsp (15 mL) toasted sesame
   seeds
1 tsp (5 mL) sesame oil
2 tbsp (30 mL) Korean hot red
   pepper paste (gochujang)

## » GUINNESS-BRAISED BEEF

MAKES 6 SERVINGS

¼ cup (60 mL) vegetable oil
3 lb (1.3 kg) flat iron (top blade)
    steak, cut into 6 pieces
3 medium yellow onions,
    chopped
3 carrots, peeled and chopped
2 stalks celery, chopped
2 heads garlic, cloves separated
    but not peeled
2 sprigs thyme
2 cans (each 440 mL) Guinness
    Stout or Draught (about
    4 cups/1 L)
4 cups (1 L) beef broth
Parsnip and Yukon Gold Mash
    (page 187)

The *Star*'s movie writer Linda Barnard discovered this refined pub dish in a Canadian-owned gastropub in New York in 2007. The Parsnip and Yukon Gold Mash (page 187) is the perfect foil for the intensity of the meat and its beer sauce. Both recipes come from chef Andy Bennett who is now cooking at a French brasserie in Arlington, Virginia. Visit a butcher for flat iron steak, a lesser-known, very beefy, well-marbled cut, or substitute flank steak.

**1.** Preheat the oven to 400°F (200°C). In a large, ovenproof pot, heat the oil over medium-high heat. Add the beef, in batches if necessary, and cook, turning once or twice, until browned on both sides, about 10 minutes. Transfer the beef to a large plate.

**2.** Add the onions, carrots, celery, garlic and thyme to the pot and cook, stirring often, until the onions are softened, about 10 minutes. Add the Guinness, bring to a boil and boil for 1 minute. Add the broth and return the beef to the pot, along with any juices that have accumulated on the plate.

**3.** Bring to a boil and cover with a lid. Transfer the pot to the oven and cook, turning the beef occasionally, until tender, about 3 hours.

**4.** Remove the beef to a plate and keep warm. Pass the braising liquid through a fine-mesh sieve, pressing on the solids to extract all the juices. Discard the solids.

**5.** Return the liquid to the pot and bring to a boil over high heat. Boil until reduced by about one-quarter and thickened slightly, 7 to 10 minutes.

**6.** To serve, divide the Parsnip and Yukon Gold Mash among 6 plates. Top each with 1 piece of beef and drizzle each portion with some of the reduced sauce.

I used to braise oversized briskets and thinly slice the meat against the grain, until I read how British chef Marco Pierre White cuts his meat into portion-sized chunks before cooking. Cut modest 4-ounce (115 g) pieces like I do for this recipe, or generous 6-ounce (170 g) ones like the chef does (in which case the brisket will divide into eight). Either way, find a butcher who will cut brisket to order. I like the fattier and more flavourful "point cut," but some prefer the leaner "flat cut."

Experiment by using different braising liquids. For beer, try Hockley Stout from Ontario or St-Ambroise Oatmeal Stout from Quebec. I serve this over quinoa, brown rice or mashed regular or sweet potatoes to sop up the braising liquid.

# EASYGOING BRISKET

MAKES 12 SERVINGS

3 lb (1.3 kg) piece beef brisket, cut into 12 pieces and patted dry

Kosher salt and/or freshly ground black pepper to taste (optional)

¼ cup (60 mL) extra virgin olive oil

6 medium yellow onions, halved and thinly sliced

4 cups (1 L) cola, stout or other dark beer, apple cider or hard cider

**1.** Preheat the oven to 325°F (160°C). If desired, season the brisket all over with salt and/or pepper.

**2.** Heat 2 tbsp (30 mL) oil in a large, ovenproof pot over medium-high heat. Cook the brisket, in batches, until well browned, about 4 minutes per side. Once browned, transfer each batch to a large plate.

**3.** Reduce the heat to medium and add the remaining 2 tbsp (30 mL) oil to the pot, along with the onions. Cook, stirring often, until softened and lightly browned, about 10 minutes.

**4.** Return the meat to the pot, along with any juices that have accumulated on the plate. Add the cola, beer or cider and bring to a boil. Cover with a lid and transfer to the oven. Cook until the meat is fork tender, 3 to 4 hours.

**5.** Either serve straight from the pot or transfer the meat and onions to a serving dish and keep warm. Bring the braising liquid to a boil over high heat and boil until it is reduced slightly, 5 to 10 minutes (this intensifies the flavours). Pour the reduced braising liquid over the meat and onions.

**6.** Serve immediately or, since braised dishes often taste better the next day, refrigerate the meat in the braising liquid overnight, then heat through gently over medium heat before serving.

## » SKILLET STEAKS WITH ANCHO ONIONS AND PEPPERS

MAKES 2 SERVINGS

**Skillet Steaks**

1 rib-eye steak cut 1-½ inches
    (4 cm) thick (about 12 to
    16 oz/340 to 450 g), patted dry
1 tsp (5 mL) kosher salt
½ tsp (2 mL) freshly ground
    black pepper
Extra virgin olive oil

**Ancho Onions and Peppers**

1 tbsp (15 mL) vegetable or extra
    virgin olive oil
1 large onion (any variety),
    halved and thinly sliced
5 large cloves garlic, chopped
2 tsp (10 mL) pure ancho chili
    powder
2 large green peppers (poblano,
    Cubanelle, Anaheim, banana
    or bell), seeded and chopped
¼ cup (60 mL) chopped
    cilantro

I swear by cast iron skillets for cooking steak. Ask your butcher to cut your meat thick so there's time to brown the outside while keeping the centre rare, and never cut open a steak to see if it's done—use the "poke test" where you press it gently with your index finger as it cooks. It will go through these stages: squishy, soft, gently yielding, slightly yielding, firm and hard. You want soft for rare, and gently yielding for medium-rare.

**1.** For the Skillet Steaks, let the meat stand at room temperature for 1 hour, then generously season it with salt and pepper and rub all over with oil.

**2.** Heat a large cast iron skillet over medium heat for 15 to 30 minutes. Add the steak to the skillet, presentation side down. Cook until the underside is golden brown, 10 to 12 minutes, reducing the heat if the meat cooks too fast and starts to blacken.

**3.** Flip the steak using tongs, then cook until the underside is golden brown, the meat is cooked rare or medium-rare and juices start to appear on the surface, about 4 minutes for medium-rare. Use the poke test to determine doneness (see above).

**4.** Remove the steak to a cutting board, cover loosely with foil and let stand for about 10 minutes, so the juices are redistributed and reabsorbed.

**5.** For the Ancho Onions and Peppers, heat the oil in the skillet over medium heat. Add the onion and garlic and cook, stirring often, until softened, about 7 minutes. Add the chili powder and cook, stirring, for 1 minute.

**6.** Add the green peppers and cook, stirring, until the vegetables are tender and lightly charred, about 6 minutes. Stir in the cilantro.

**7.** To serve, slice the steak thickly on the diagonal, then divide the steak and vegetables between 2 plates.

I lucked into this recipe while preparing a story about Foodstock, a momentous gathering of more than 20,000 chefs, farmers and citizens on a farm northwest of Orangeville in October 2011 to protest about a proposed mega quarry.

Carl Cosack, vice-chair of a group opposed to the quarry, shared the recipe. He's a rancher who runs Rawhide Adventures (rawhide-adventures.on.ca) at his Peace Valley Ranch and goes by the nickname Crusty. He cooks his steak on a campfire but you could barbecue yours.

**1.** Let the steak stand at room temperature for 30 to 60 minutes, then pat dry with paper towels. Sprinkle with salt and pepper to taste and rub with oil.

**2.** Heat a large cast iron skillet over medium heat for at least 15 minutes. Add the steak and cook until the underside is well browned, about 8 minutes. Flip the steak with tongs, then cook until the underside is golden brown, the meat is cooked rare or medium-rare and juices start to appear on the surface, about 4 minutes for medium-rare.

**3.** Meanwhile for the Steak Sauce, whisk together the vinegar, ketchup, maple syrup, Worcestershire sauce, garlic, cumin and pepper in a small bowl.

**4.** When the steak is ready, transfer it to a shallow dish just large enough to hold it. Pour the Steak Sauce over the steak, cover the dish tightly with foil or a lid and let stand for 10 minutes.

**5.** Remove the steak from the dish and pour the Steak Sauce and any accumulated juices from the steak into a gravy boat. Thinly slice the steak against the grain, arrange the slices on a serving platter and pass the sauce separately.

# TRAIL BOSS'S JUICY SIRLOIN  «

MAKES 6 SERVINGS

**Steak**
1-½ lb (680 g) top sirloin (at least 1 inch/2.5 cm thick)
Kosher salt and freshly ground black pepper to taste
Extra virgin olive oil to taste

**Steak Sauce**
3 tbsp (45 mL) cider vinegar
2 tbsp (30 mL) ketchup
1 tbsp (15 mL) pure maple syrup
1 tbsp (15 mL) Worcestershire sauce
1 clove garlic, minced
½ tsp (2 mL) ground cumin
¼ tsp (1 mL) freshly ground black pepper

## » KOREAN BEEF SHORT RIBS

## (GALBI)

MAKES ABOUT 6 SERVINGS

1 Asian pear, peeled, cored and
   grated or puréed
½ medium yellow onion, grated
   or puréed
⅓ cup (80 mL) soy sauce
3 tbsp (45 mL) packed light
   brown sugar
3 tbsp (45 mL) sesame oil
3 tbsp (45 mL) mirin (Japanese
   sweet rice cooking wine)
2 tbsp (30 mL) toasted sesame
   seeds
1 tbsp (15 mL) minced garlic
½ tsp (2 mL) freshly ground
   black pepper
3 lb (1.3 kg) Korean beef short
   ribs (galbi or LA galbi), cut
   into ¼-inch (6 mm) thick
   pieces that are about 8 inches
   (20 cm) long and have about
   3 bones
Vegetable oil for cooking

This is one of the top three Korean restaurant dishes in Canada (along with bulgogi and bibimbap which are on pages 111 and 113 respectively) and is easy to make at home if you visit a Korean supermarket for the pre-sliced meat (see My Favourite Places to Shop, page 228). The short ribs are cut very thinly across the bone so they cook quickly. I use a cast iron skillet for the short ribs but you can barbecue them if you prefer.

**1.** In a large bowl, stir together the pear, onion, soy sauce, sugar, sesame oil, mirin, sesame seeds, garlic and pepper. Add the meat and mix well. Cover and refrigerate, stirring occasionally, for at least 3 hours or overnight. (Alternatively, combine everything in a large, resealable plastic bag then refrigerate, turning the bag occasionally.)

**2.** When ready to cook, remove the meat from the marinade, discarding the marinade. Heat a large, lightly oiled cast iron skillet over medium-high heat. Cook the ribs, in batches, for about 3 minutes per side or to the desired doneness.

Naomi Green, a.k.a. Miss Sonia, co-owns Diners Corner (diners-corner.com), a West Indian/Chinese/Canadian restaurant. When I profiled Naomi in 2003 for a series called *Inner Chef*, she shared this Jamaican oxtail recipe. Oxtail, which is actually beef tail, is bony and tough but becomes flavourful and tender when braised. Look for it in Asian supermarkets, butcher shops and some supermarkets. You'll find seasoning salt in bulk food stores.

# MISS SONIA'S JAMAICAN OXTAIL

«

MAKES 2 SERVINGS

2 lb (900 g) oxtail pieces, washed
1 large yellow onion, halved and thinly sliced
½ green Scotch bonnet chili, seeded and minced
2 tbsp (30 mL) mushroom soy sauce
2 tbsp (30 mL) vegetable oil
1 tbsp (15 mL) minced or puréed garlic
1 tbsp (15 mL) seasoning salt
4 sprigs thyme
¼ tsp (1 mL) freshly ground black pepper
1-½ cups (375 mL) water
Steamed rice for serving (optional)

**1.** In a large bowl, toss the oxtail with the onion, chili, soy sauce, oil, garlic, seasoning salt, thyme and pepper. Let stand at room temperature for 30 minutes.

**2.** Transfer the contents of the bowl to a large pot and add the water. Bring to a boil over high heat. Reduce the heat to medium-low and simmer, covered, until the oxtail is tender, about 90 minutes.

**3.** Discard the thyme sprigs and serve the oxtail with its gravy, and rice, if desired.

## » SMOKED PAPRIKA-CRUSTED MARROW BONES

MAKES 4 SERVINGS

**Marrow Bones**
Kosher salt (optional)
8 pieces split beef marrow
    bones, cut into 5- to 7-inch
    (13 to 18 cm) lengths
Extra virgin olive oil to taste
Minced garlic to taste
Rosemary or thyme sprigs to
    taste
Smoked paprika to taste

**Parsley Salad**
½ cup (125 mL) flat-leaf parsley
    leaves
¼ cup (60 mL) freshly grated,
    peeled horseradish
4 tsp (20 mL) fresh lemon juice
4 tsp (20 mL) extra virgin olive
    oil
½ tsp kosher salt, or to taste
1 baguette, sliced, or 8 slices
    toast, crusts removed, cut
    into thick slices, for serving
Flaky sea salt for sprinkling
    (optional)

We've long enjoyed the marrow in osso buco (Italian braised veal shanks), but it was only in recent years that chefs turned us on to roasted beef marrow bones. Toronto chef Scott Vivian showed me how to make his version that's on the menu at his restaurant Beast (thebeastrestaurant.com). As I wrote in 2010, "slathered on bread or toast, it's a primal yet luxurious feast." Get marrow bones from butcher shops and some supermarkets.

**1.** For the marrow bones, if time allows, fill a large bowl or pot with cold water and whisk in 2 tbsp (30 mL) salt until it has dissolved. Add the marrow bones and let them soak in the fridge for up to 24 hours (this draws the blood out), changing the water several times and adding more salt each time. Rinse the bones and pat them dry. Let stand at room temperature for 1 hour.

**2.** Preheat the oven to 325°F (160°F). Arrange the bones, cut sides up, on a baking sheet. Drizzle the tops with oil. Sprinkle with garlic and lay a few rosemary or thyme sprigs on top. Bake in the centre of the oven until the marrow is hot, soft and starting to separate from the bone but not melting, 15 to 20 minutes.

**3.** Discard the herbs and sprinkle the bones generously with smoked paprika. Switch the oven to broil, then broil the bones under high heat on the upper oven rack for 2 minutes.

**4.** Meanwhile, for the Parsley Salad, toss together the parsley, horseradish, lemon juice, oil and salt in a serving bowl.

**5.** To serve, arrange 1 to 2 bones on each plate. Pass the Parsley Salad, bread and sea salt (if using) separately. To eat, scoop out the marrow from the bones with a spoon or knife, spread it on the bread, sprinkle with salt (if using) and top with a little of the Parsley Salad.

When the hit movie *My Big Fat Greek Wedding* was released in 2003, I enjoyed a cooking lesson at Ellas Banquet Hall & Hospitality Centre (ellas.com), when it had a restaurant in Toronto's Greektown, and I learned how to make this mouth-watering lamb rack. Buy the meatiest racks you can find. The restaurant favours Ontario lamb and so do I. Knife-sharpening steels (also called butcher's steels) are long, thin and round, usually with pointed ends. If you don't have one, use a long, slim knife to hollow out the lamb rack.

# RACK OF LAMB STUFFED WITH CHEESE AND HERBS

MAKES 4–6 SERVINGS

2 large 8-bone lamb racks (each about 1-½ lb/680 g), fat trimmed
2 tbsp (30 mL) ricotta
2 tbsp (30 mL) grated feta cheese
2 tbsp (30 mL) grated kefalotiri or Romano cheese
1 tsp (5 mL) dried oregano, plus more for sprinkling
1 tsp (5 mL) dried thyme, plus more for sprinkling
Water as needed
Extra virgin olive oil to taste

**1.** Preheat the oven to 400°F (200°C). Cut the lamb racks in half crosswise to make four, 4-bone racks. Using the pointed end of a knife-sharpening steel, poke a hole about a finger's width through the meaty part of each lamb rack. Alternatively, use a long, slim knife to cut a small X through the centre of the meat.

**2.** In a medium bowl, mix together the ricotta, feta, kefalotiri or Romano, 1 tsp (5 mL) oregano and 1 tsp (5 mL) thyme. Using your fingers, stuff the lamb racks with equal amounts of the cheese mixture.

**3.** Put the lamb racks, bone sides down, in a shallow roasting pan and add enough water to just cover the bottom of the pan. Drizzle the meaty parts of the racks with oil, rubbing it in well with your hands. Sprinkle the top of each rack with thyme and oregano to taste. Roast in the oven for about 20 minutes for rare, 25 minutes for medium.

**4.** Transfer the lamb racks to a cutting board and let stand, loosely covered with foil, for 5 minutes before carving into individual chops.

## » LUCK-OF-THE-BREWERS LAMB STEW

MAKES 4-6 SERVINGS

2-½ lb (1.1 kg) boneless lamb shoulder or leg, cut into 1-inch (2.5 cm) cubes and patted dry

Kosher salt and freshly ground black pepper to taste

2 tbsp (30 mL) extra virgin olive oil, plus more if needed

2 medium yellow onions, diced

2 carrots, peeled and diced

2 stalks celery, diced

2 large cloves garlic, minced

1 tbsp (15 mL) all-purpose flour

¼ cup (60 mL) dry white wine

1 bottle (341 mL) dark lager, such as Waterloo Dark or Smoked Oatmeal Stout

3 cups (750 mL) chicken or vegetable broth

10 fingerling potatoes, halved lengthwise or 12 oz (340 g) small, yellow-flesh potatoes, halved

8 oz (225 g) shiitake mushrooms, stems removed and caps thinly sliced

1 tbsp (15 mL) crème fraîche

1 tsp (5 mL) drained, prepared horseradish

My go-to lamb stew celebrates Ontario lamb, fingerling potatoes and shiitake mushrooms. It's delicious as is but stirring in crème fraîche and horseradish at the end takes it to another level. Chef Ezra Title, who runs Toronto catering company Chezvous Dining (chezvousdining.ca), created this stew for the Ontario Craft Brewers (ontariocraftbrewers.com) for St. Patrick's Day in 2008.

**1.** Season the lamb with salt and pepper. In a large pot, heat 1 tbsp (15 mL) oil over medium-high heat. In 2 batches, brown the lamb on all sides, about 8 minutes per batch. Transfer the lamb to a large plate as each batch browns.

**2.** Add the onions, carrots, celery and garlic to the pot and cook over medium-high heat, stirring often, until softened, about 5 minutes, adding a little more oil if the pot is too dry. Add the flour and cook, stirring, for 2 minutes.

**3.** Add the wine and cook, stirring, until it evaporates. Add the beer and bring to a boil, scraping up any brown bits from the bottom of the pot. Reduce the heat to medium and simmer for 5 minutes.

**4.** Add the broth and return the lamb to the pot, along with any juices that have accumulated on the plate. Bring to a boil over high heat. Reduce the heat to medium, then simmer briskly, uncovered, until the lamb is fork tender, about 45 minutes. Add the potatoes and simmer, uncovered, until tender, about 25 minutes.

**5.** Meanwhile, heat the remaining 1 tbsp (15 mL) oil in a medium skillet over medium-high heat. Add the mushrooms and cook, stirring often, until the mushrooms release and reabsorb their juices, about 8 minutes.

**6.** Stir the mushrooms into the stew, along with the crème fraîche and horseradish.

The highlight of 2011 was a trip to Sudbury for porketta bingo, a card game played at the Beef 'n Bird tavern on Saturday afternoons for meat instead of money. Win a round and you get bread and a pound of hot porketta, a Canadian spin on Italian porchetta and the northern city's signature dish.

Various chefs and butchers, including Dominic Nesci of D&A Fine Meats, showed me how to make the traditional dill-and-garlic-stuffed porketta. At Vespa Street Kitchen (ribsupperclub.com), Robert Gregorini seasons his porketta with fennel instead of dill.

It's hard to find pork roasts with skin so you might have to order one from a butcher. Buy fennel pollen (the intense and distinctive-tasting small, dried petals and pollen of the wild fennel flower) from the Spice Trader (thespicetrader.ca) or Just A Pinch (justapinch.ca).

**1.** Preheat the oven to 325°F (160°C). With a sharp knife, score the pork skin in a cross-hatch, diamond pattern. If your butcher hasn't butterflied the roast, slice the pork in half horizontally nearly all the way so it opens like a book. Lightly score the inside flesh with the knife.

**2.** For the Porketta with Dill and Garlic, stir together the garlic, dill weed, dill seed, salt and pepper in a small bowl. Spread the mixture all over the inside of the pork, massaging it into the crevices.

**3.** For the Porketta with Fennel, combine the garlic, oil and salt in a mini food processor and process to form a paste. Spread the paste all over the inside of the pork, massaging it into the crevices. In a coffee grinder reserved for spices, grind the fennel seeds and fennel pollen (if using) to form a powder. Stir in the red chili flakes.

Sprinkle evenly over the garlic paste on the pork.

**4.** For either version, close the pork so the skin is on the top. Tie the pork tightly with butcher's twine. Put the pork, skin side up, on a rack in a shallow roasting pan and pour the water into the pan.

**5.** Roast in the oven until the internal temperature reaches 170°F (77°C), about 3 hours, basting occasionally with the pan juices. If the skin isn't crisp enough, increase the heat to 425°F (220°C) and roast until the skin is crisp and browned, about 10 to 15 minutes, watching closely.

**6.** Remove the pork from the oven, cover loosely with foil and let stand for 15 minutes before carving.

# SUDBURY PORKETTA TWO WAYS  «

MAKES ABOUT 8 SERVINGS

4 lb (1.8 kg) skin-on, boneless pork shoulder blade roast, butterflied
½ cup (125 mL) water

**Porketta with Dill and Garlic**
6 large cloves garlic, minced
2 tbsp (30 mL) dried dill weed
2 tbsp (30 mL) dried dill seed
2 tsp (10 mL) kosher salt
2 tsp (10 mL) cracked or coarsely ground black pepper

**Porketta with Fennel**
Peeled cloves from 1 head garlic
2-½ tbsp (37 mL) extra virgin olive oil
½ tsp (2 mL) kosher salt
2 tbsp (30 mL) fennel seeds
½ tsp (2 mL) fennel pollen (optional)
½ tsp (2 mL) dried red chili flakes

## » TONKATSU

### (PANKO PORK CUTLETS)

MAKES 4 SERVINGS

**Pork Cutlets**

3 tbsp (45 mL) all-purpose flour
Kosher salt and freshly ground
    black pepper to taste
1 large egg
1 cup (250 mL) panko (Japanese
    coarse dried bread crumbs)
4 thin, boneless pork chops
    (about 1 lb/450 g total),
    patted dry
Vegetable oil for frying

**Quick Tonkatsu Sauce**

¼ cup (60 mL) Worcestershire
    sauce or A.1. steak sauce
1 tbsp (15 mL) ketchup
Pinch granulated sugar

Tonkatsu is the sublime Japanese version of a breaded, pan-fried pork cutlet which is usually served sliced with short-grain white rice and miso soup. Cheap, thin, fast-fry supermarket chops are best for this dish but if they're too thick, pound them with a meat mallet or heavy saucepan before cooking. You can buy Bulldog brand tonkatsu sauce or make my cheater's version. To turn tonkatsu into katsu kare (pork cutlet with curry sauce), make the Japanese Curry with Vegetables (page 147) and serve it with rice alongside the chops.

**1.** For the pork cutlets, put the flour on a large plate and season it with salt and pepper. Put the egg in a shallow bowl and beat it lightly with a fork. Put the panko on a second large plate.

**2.** Coat each pork chop in flour, then in egg, then in panko to coat completely. Transfer the chops to a clean plate until ready to cook.

**3.** In a medium skillet, heat about ½ inch (1 cm) oil over medium-high heat. If you have a heatproof thermometer, heat the oil to 350°F (180°C). If not, heat the oil until a piece of panko floats and browns without sinking.

**4.** Cook the chops 2 at a time until golden, crispy and cooked through, about 3 minutes per side, reducing the heat slightly if the chops brown too fast. Using tongs, transfer the chops to a wire rack set over paper towels to drain. Let the oil reheat before you cook the remaining pork chops.

**5.** For the Quick Tonkatsu Sauce, whisk together the Worcestershire or steak sauce, ketchup and sugar in a small bowl.

**6.** To serve, slice the chops thickly on the diagonal and serve with Quick Tonkatsu Sauce.

## » GAMJATANG

### (PORK BONE SOUP)

MAKES 6 SERVINGS

4 lb (1.8 kg) meaty pork neck
    bones
5 thin slices ginger
12 cups (3 L) water
1 medium yellow onion, halved
    and thinly sliced
2 tbsp (30 mL) Korean hot red
    pepper paste (gochujang)
2 tbsp (30 mL) Korean soybean
    paste
10 small dried red chilies (each 1
    to 2 inches/2.5 to 5 cm)
8 large cloves garlic, minced
3 tbsp (45 mL) green perilla
    seeds, plus more for optional
    garnish
2 tbsp (30 mL) Korean coarse
    red pepper powder
1 tbsp (15 mL) minced, peeled
    ginger
¼ napa cabbage, cored and
    chopped
4 large white potatoes, peeled
    and quartered
12 fresh perilla (shiso) leaves,
    sliced into thick strips
    (optional)
3 tbsp (45 mL) Asian fish sauce
    or Korean anchovy sauce
    (optional)
Kosher salt to taste (optional)
4 green onions, thinly sliced
Steamed medium-grain rice for
    serving

Jinah Choi, the head chef at Galleria Supermarket (galleriasm.com) in Toronto and Thornhill, taught me how to make this pork dish, a cheap and popular meal at Korean restaurants. (Four pounds of meaty bones should cost less than $6.) It's called a soup but is really a big bowl of meaty pork bones that you pick at with your fingers, served with potatoes and rice. It's hearty and fun to eat.

**1.** If time allows, soak the bones in a large pot or bowl of water for at least 2 hours or overnight in the fridge, changing the water several times (this helps draw out the blood from the bones). Drain the bones and rinse them in cold water.

**2.** Bring a large pot of water to a boil over high heat. Add the bones and ginger slices and cook for 7 minutes. Drain, discarding the ginger.

**3.** Rinse the bones and return them to the pot. Add 12 cups (3 L) water, the yellow onion, hot red pepper paste, soybean paste and dried chilies. Bring to a boil over high heat. Reduce the heat to medium and simmer briskly, covered, for 1 hour, adding more water or reducing the heat if the water seems to evaporate too quickly.

**4.** Stir in the garlic, 3 tbsp (45 mL) perilla seeds, the red pepper powder and minced ginger. Reduce the heat to low and simmer, covered, for 1 hour.

**5.** Meanwhile, bring a medium saucepan of water to a boil over high heat. Add the cabbage and cook for 2 minutes. Drain the cabbage and rinse with cold water. Squeeze out any excess water from the cabbage and add it to the pot, along with the potatoes.

**6.** Increase the heat to medium and cook, covered, until the potatoes are fork tender but not falling apart, about 30 minutes. Stir in the perilla leaves (if using). Taste and stir in the fish sauce or anchovy sauce, if using, or salt.

**7.** To serve, divide the pork bones and potatoes among 6 large bowls and ladle in broth to taste, discarding the dried red chilies. Sprinkle with green onions and perilla seeds (if using). Serve each bowl with chopsticks, a large soup spoon and a bowl of rice alongside.

**8.** To eat, use the chopsticks to pick the meat off the bones, and the spoon for the broth and potatoes, spooning the rice into the broth, as desired. Provide an empty bowl for the discarded bones.

Cookbook author and cooking instructor Smita Chandra (smitachandra.com) and her husband, Sanjeev, made six chicken curries for us in 2007. This classic recipe from Punjab is close to what you'll find on most North Indian restaurant menus in Toronto.

1. In a food processor, combine the onion, garlic, ginger and green chili (if using) and pulse until finely minced.

2. In a large non-stick skillet or large, shallow saucepan, heat the oil over medium-high heat. Add the cumin seeds and cook for a few seconds until they begin to pop. Add the onion mixture and cook, stirring often, until the onion is lightly browned, 7 to 8 minutes.

3. Reduce the heat to medium and add the tomatoes. Cook until the liquid has evaporated and the mixture has thickened slightly, about 5 minutes.

4. Add the sour cream and cook, stirring, for 5 minutes. Add the coriander, ground cumin, fenugreek, turmeric, garam masala, cayenne and black pepper, and cook, stirring, for 1 minute.

5. Add the chicken to the skillet, stirring to coat well with the sauce. Increase the heat to high and bring to a boil. Reduce the heat to medium-low and cook, covered, stirring occasionally, until the chicken is tender and no longer pink inside, about 30 minutes. (The chicken will release its juices and create a gravy.)

6. Stir in the cilantro and lemon juice and serve with rice, if desired.

# SMITA CHANDRA'S CLASSIC CHICKEN CURRY

«

MAKES 4 SERVINGS

1 medium yellow onion, quartered
2 cloves garlic, peeled
½-inch (1 cm) piece ginger, peeled
1 small, thin, fresh green chili, stem removed (optional)
2 tbsp (30 mL) vegetable oil
½ tsp (2 mL) cumin seeds
6 drained canned plum tomatoes, puréed (about 1 cup/250 mL)
3 tbsp (45 mL) sour cream
1 tsp (5 mL) ground coriander
1 tsp (5 mL) ground cumin
1 tsp (5 mL) dried fenugreek leaves
½ tsp (2 mL) turmeric
½ tsp (2 mL) garam masala
¼ to ½ tsp (1 to 2 mL) cayenne, to taste
¼ tsp (1 mL) freshly ground black pepper
10 boneless, skinless chicken thighs (about 1-½ lb/680 g), cut into bite-size pieces
2 tbsp (30 mL) chopped cilantro
1 tbsp (15 mL) fresh lemon juice
Steamed brown or white basmati rice (optional) for serving

## » CHICKEN KAT-A-KAT

MAKES 4–6 SERVINGS

3 tbsp (45 mL) vegetable oil or
  ghee (clarified butter)
1 medium yellow onion, finely
  diced
2 tbsp (30 mL) minced garlic
2 tbsp (30 mL) minced, peeled
  ginger
1 package (1.75 oz/50 g) kat-a-
  kat masala, or to taste
2 lb (900 g) boneless, skinless
  chicken (preferably a mix of
  breast and thigh meat), finely
  diced
2 medium tomatoes, finely diced
5 green chilies (each about
  3 inches/7.5 cm), with seeds,
  minced (or more to taste)
1 cup (250 mL) chopped
  cilantro
3 tbsp (45 mL) plain yogurt

Kat-a-kat, one of Pakistan's beloved dishes, is usually made with offal such as brain, heart and kidney. At Touch of Spice (touchofspice.ca) in Mississauga, owner Mohammed (Moe) Shaikh has reimagined the dish with white and dark chicken meat that's diced small enough to start to shred during cooking.

Mohammed uses Shan Foods brand kat-a-kat masala, a blend of chilies, aniseed, garlic and other spices that comes in ½-cup (125 mL) packages. It's a flavourful, spicy masala so feel free to use less. Serve the chicken with steamed basmati rice or an Indian bread such as naan.

**1.** In a large saucepan, heat the oil or ghee over medium-high heat. Add the onion, garlic and ginger, and cook, stirring often, for 4 minutes. Add the kat-a-kat masala and cook, stirring, for 2 minutes.

**2.** Add the chicken, tomatoes and chilies, and cook, stirring often, until the chicken releases and reabsorbs its juices and is no longer pink inside, and the mixture is nearly dry, 8 to 12 minutes.

**3.** Remove the saucepan from the heat and stir in the cilantro and yogurt.

For a 2011 Mother's Day story called "Three hot mamas (and one hot nonna)," I asked Toronto chefs and their moms to cook for me. At the Black Skirt (blackskirtrestaurant.com), chef Rosa Gallé reverted to the role of daughter and let her mom, Tommasina Gallé, make this home-style Italian chicken.

# CHICKEN PIZZAIOLO &laquo;

4 boneless, skinless single
   chicken breasts
½ cup (125 mL) All-Purpose
   Tomato Sauce (page 181) or
   purchased tomato sauce
½ cup (125 mL) vegetable oil
¼ cup (60 mL) water
2 large cloves garlic, lightly
   smashed
1 large sprig rosemary, leaves
   chopped and stem discarded
2 tbsp (30 mL) chopped flat-leaf
   parsley
¼ tsp (1 mL) dried thyme
Kosher salt to taste
Crusty Italian bread for serving
   (optional)

**1.** Put the chicken breasts on a large cutting board between 2 pieces of plastic wrap. Using a meat mallet or pounder, or the bottom of a heavy can or skillet, pound the breasts as thinly as possible.

**2.** In a large, wide non-stick skillet over medium heat, combine the tomato sauce, oil, water, garlic, rosemary, 1 tbsp (15 mL) parsley and the thyme. Cook, stirring, for 3 minutes until bubbling.

**3.** Add the chicken breasts to the skillet in a single layer and sprinkle with salt to taste. Cover the skillet with a lid and cook until the chicken is no longer pink inside, 5 to 7 minutes, depending on the thickness of the breasts.

**4.** Remove the lid and increase the heat to high. Cook, uncovered, for 2 minutes to thicken the sauce slightly.

**5.** Transfer the chicken to a large, shallow serving dish. Pour the tomato sauce over the chicken and sprinkle with the remaining 1 tbsp (15 mL) parsley. If desired, serve with bread for mopping up the sauce.

When New York writer Grace Young (graceyoung.com) released *Stir-Frying to the Sky's Edge: The Ultimate Guide to Mastery, with Authentic Recipes and Stories* (Simon & Schuster, 2010), the book inspired me to buy my first carbon-steel wok (14 inches/36 cm as directed) from Chan Chi Kee Cutlery in Pacific Mall. For just $20, I now have the perfect tool for restaurant-quality stir-fries.

I love how aromatic Sichuan peppercorns, the berries of the prickly ash tree that's part of the lemon family, make your mouth tingle in this flavourful stir-fry. Serve it with steamed rice.

**1.** Put the Sichuan peppercorns in a large wok or skillet, discarding any tiny stems. Toast over medium-low heat until fragrant, about 4 minutes. Remove the peppercorns from the wok and let cool slightly, then grind finely in a coffee grinder reserved for spices.

**2.** In a medium bowl, stir together the chicken, ginger, garlic, cornstarch, light soy sauce, sugar and 1 tsp (5 mL) rice wine.

**3.** In a small bowl, stir together the broth or water, vinegar, dark soy sauce, sesame oil and remaining 1 tbsp (15 mL) rice wine.

**4.** Heat a wok or large skillet over high heat. Add 1 tbsp (15 mL) peanut or vegetable oil, swirling to coat the entire surface. Add the chilies and Sichuan pepper and stir-fry just until the chilies begin to smoke, 5 to 10 seconds.

**5.** Push the chili mixture to one side of the wok and add the chicken mixture in 1 layer. Cook the chicken, undisturbed, for 1 minute, then stir-fry until lightly browned but not cooked through, about 1 minute.

**6.** Swirl in the remaining 1 tbsp (15 mL) peanut or vegetable oil. Add the bell pepper and stir-fry for 1 minute. Add the broth mixture and stir-fry until the chicken is no longer pink inside, about 1 minute. Add the cashews and green onions and stir-fry for 1 minute.

# SICHUAN PEPPERCORN-CASHEW CHICKEN

### MAKES 4 SERVINGS

¾ tsp (4 mL) Sichuan peppercorns (sometimes labelled prickly ash)

1 lb (450 g) boneless, skinless chicken thighs, cut into ½-inch (1 cm) pieces

2 tbsp (30 mL) peeled, minced ginger

2 tbsp (30 mL) minced garlic

1 tbsp (15 mL) cornstarch

2 tsp (10 mL) light soy sauce

2 tsp (10 mL) granulated sugar

1 tsp (5 mL) plus 1 tbsp (15 mL) Shao Hsing rice wine

2 tbsp (30 mL) chicken broth or water

1 tbsp (15 mL) Chinkiang vinegar (black rice vinegar)

1 tsp (5 mL) dark soy sauce

1 tsp (5 mL) sesame oil

2 tbsp (30 mL) peanut or vegetable oil

10 small dried red chilies (each about 2 inches/5 cm long)

1 red bell pepper, seeded and cut into ½-inch (1 cm) pieces

¾ cup (185 mL) roasted, unsalted cashews

4 green onions, cut into 1-inch (2.5 cm) pieces

## » YUKIGUNI'S YAKITORI

### (CHICKEN AND GREEN ONION SKEWERS)

MAKES 12 (SERVING 4)

12 bamboo or wooden skewers
    (8 inches/20 cm long)
2 tbsp (30 mL) cold water
1 tsp (5 mL) cornstarch
¼ cup (60 mL) mirin (Japanese
    sweet rice cooking wine)
¼ cup (60 mL) light soy sauce
4 tsp (20 mL) granulated sugar
1 lb (450 g) boneless, skinless
    chicken thighs, cut into
    1-inch (2.5 cm) chunks
1 bunch green onions (dark and
    light green parts only), cut
    into 1-inch (2.5 cm) pieces
Kosher salt and freshly ground
    black pepper to taste

Freelance writer Cynthia David (cynthia-david.com) went to Niagara Falls in 2004 to check on the Japanese restaurant scene and came back with these soy-glazed chicken skewers from Yukiguni restaurant (yukiguni.ca), now owned by Noriyuki Ricky Kikuchi. You can opt for metal, instead of bamboo, skewers and a barbecue (preferably charcoal) instead of the broiler.

**1.** Soak the skewers in a bowl of hot water for at least 1 hour.

**2.** In a small bowl, whisk together 2 tbsp (30 mL) water and cornstarch until smooth.

**3.** In a small saucepan, bring the mirin, soy sauce and sugar to a boil over medium heat. Add the cornstarch mixture and cook, stirring constantly, until the mixture is thick and clear with no taste of cornstarch, about 3 minutes. Remove the saucepan from the heat and set aside.

**4.** Preheat the broiler to high. Thread the chicken chunks and green onion pieces alternately onto the soaked skewers, dividing evenly. Sprinkle with salt and pepper.

**5.** Put the skewers on a baking sheet and broil for 8 minutes, turning often. Brush all over with the soy glaze and continue to broil until the chicken is golden on the outside and no longer pink inside, about 2 minutes. Brush again with the soy glaze just before serving.

I learned to make the national dish of the Philippines from Mayette Morillo, who runs Mayette's Fine Foods (mayettes.ca), a Filipino restaurant in Toronto's east end. This easy braise is also good with cubed pork shoulder and, either way, it's best served with steamed white rice.

# CHICKEN ADOBO ≪

MAKES 4 SERVINGS

4 chicken legs, cut into thighs
    and drumsticks, skin
    removed from thighs
½ cup (125 mL) white vinegar
⅓ cup (80 mL) soy sauce
2 tbsp (30 mL) minced garlic
3 bay leaves
½ tsp (2 mL) freshly ground
    black pepper
½ cup (125 mL) water
1 tbsp (15 mL) vegetable oil

**1.** In a large bowl or resealable plastic bag, combine the chicken, vinegar, soy sauce, 1 tbsp (15 mL) garlic, the bay leaves and pepper, and mix well. Cover, or seal the bag, then refrigerate for at least 1 hour or overnight, stirring, or turning the bag, occasionally.

**2.** Pour the chicken and its marinade into a large saucepan and add the water. Bring to a boil over high heat. Reduce the heat to medium-low and simmer, covered, until the chicken is tender, 45 to 60 minutes.

**3.** With a slotted spoon, remove the chicken to a large bowl, reserving the cooking liquid in the saucepan. Cover the chicken and keep warm.

**4.** In a large non-stick skillet, heat the oil over medium-high heat. Add the remaining 1 tbsp (15 mL) garlic and cook, stirring, until browned, 1 to 2 minutes.

**5.** Add the chicken to the skillet in a single layer, and cook until browned on both sides, about 4 minutes, turning once. Add the reserved cooking liquid to the saucepan. Bring to a simmer and cook for 2 minutes. Discard the bay leaves and transfer the chicken and the sauce to a serving dish.

## » JUICY, CRISPY, FENNEL-SCENTED CHICKEN THIGHS

MAKES 6 SERVINGS

3 tbsp (45 mL) Dijon mustard

3 tbsp (45 mL) light soy sauce

2 tbsp (30 mL) fresh lemon juice

1 tbsp (15 mL) extra virgin olive oil

6 bone-in, skin-on chicken thighs

1 tbsp (15 mL) dried thyme

1 tsp (5 mL) fennel seeds

Freshly ground black pepper to taste

About ½ cup (125 mL) chicken broth, as needed

"What a great way to use cheap chicken to make a weekly meal!"

**MICHELLE CLERMONT,** LONDON, ONT.

"I was so pleased with the result. The lemon juice, Dijon mustard, soy sauce and fennel seeds make it special."

**MARIE KIRCHMEIR,** BLIND RIVER, ONT.

Cooking inexpensive chicken thighs slowly in a flavour-packed broth results in moist meat and crispy, herbed skin. I've adapted this reader favourite from a recipe I reviewed in *Cristina Ferrare's Big Bowl of Love: Delight Family and Friends with More Than 150 Simple, Fabulous Recipes* (Sterling Epicure, 2011).

**1.** Preheat the oven to 350°F (180°C). In an 8-inch (2 L) square baking dish, whisk together the Dijon, soy sauce, lemon juice and oil. Add the chicken thighs, turning them several times to coat in the mustard mixture.

**2.** Arrange the thighs in a single layer in the dish, sprinkle the tops with thyme and fennel and season generously with pepper. Cover the dish with foil and bake in the oven for 45 minutes.

**3.** Remove the foil and baste the chicken thighs with the juices in the dish. Add the broth as needed so only the tops of the chicken thighs remain exposed, and the rest is submerged in liquid. Roast, uncovered, for 1 hour. The skin will be browned and crispy and the meat moist and tender.

**4.** Transfer the chicken thighs to a platter. Pour the juices from the dish into a gravy boat and serve with the chicken.

I grew up fishing for pickerel, bass and lake trout in northern Ontario, and when my parents retired they bought a home on Lake Nipissing so my dad, Harry, could fish pickerel in summer and winter. This is how my mom, Barbara, always cooks it, and I can barely eat pickerel any other way.

# MY MOM'S PAN-FRIED PICKEREL

MAKES 4-6 SERVINGS

20 soda crackers (salted or unsalted)
1 large egg
1 tbsp (15 mL) water
8 boneless, skinless pickerel fillets (each 4 to 6 oz/115 to 170 g), patted dry
Canola oil for frying
Lemon wedges for serving

**1.** Preheat the oven to 200°F (100°C). In a food processor, pulse the crackers until fine crumbs form. Spread the crumbs out on a large plate or put them in a sturdy plastic bag. In a shallow dish, whisk together the egg and water.

**2.** Working with 1 fillet at a time, dip each pickerel fillet in the egg mixture, letting the excess drip off. Either lay each fillet in the cracker crumbs, turning to coat, or add the fillets, 1 at a time, to the bag of crumbs and shake gently to coat. As each fillet is coated, lay it on a large plate.

**3.** In a medium cast iron or other heavy skillet, heat ¼ inch (6 mm) oil over high heat. Add 2 fillets at a time to the skillet and cook until the undersides are browned, 45 to 60 seconds. Carefully flip the fillets with a spatula and cook until golden, 45 to 60 seconds.

**4.** Remove the fillets to a wire rack set over a baking sheet and transfer to the oven to keep warm while you cook the remaining fillets. Serve the pickerel with lemon wedges for squeezing over the top.

## » BAKED COD WITH GARLIC-HERB PANKO CRUST

MAKES 4 SERVINGS

1-½ lb (680 g) cod fillets (about 1-inch/2.5 cm thick at the wider end), cut into 4 pieces and patted dry
2 tbsp (30 mL) extra virgin olive oil
Fine sea salt and freshly ground black pepper to taste
¼ cup (60 mL) panko (Japanese coarse dried bread crumbs)
¼ cup (60 mL) finely chopped flat-leaf parsley
2 large cloves garlic, minced
4 tsp (20 mL) unsalted butter, cut into 12 small cubes

In 2009, food writer Susan Sampson detailed how Cooke Aquaculture in the Maritimes had begun farming Atlantic cod and hoped to eventually sell its fish. In the meantime, chef Chris Aerni, owner of the Rossmount Inn (rossmountinn.com) in St. Andrews, New Brunswick, has been serving the farmed cod and developing recipes. You'll probably have to buy wild cod until the farmed variety reaches the stores, but you can use any firm white-fleshed fish for this recipe.

**1.** Preheat the oven to 400°F (200°C). Line a large baking sheet with parchment paper or lightly oil it.

**2.** Brush the cod fillets on both sides with oil, then sprinkle with salt and pepper. Put the fillets in a single layer on the prepared baking sheet.

**3.** In a small bowl, mix together the panko, parsley and garlic, and sprinkle evenly over the fillets. Dot the fillets with the butter.

**4.** Bake on the upper-middle rack of the oven until the cod fillets barely flake with a fork, 8 to 9 minutes. If desired, turn the oven to broil and broil under high heat for 1 minute to crisp the topping.

When I want a flavour-packed, well-balanced meal that comes together quickly and effortlessly on a work night, I turn to fish. For this recipe I often use those portion-size pieces of salmon from the supermarket, but when I have time I buy Arctic char or rainbow trout fillets from a fishmonger (discarding the skin after baking).

## A SIMPLE SALMON SUPPER

«

MAKES 2 SERVINGS

**1.** Preheat the oven to 450°F (230°C). Line a baking sheet with parchment paper.

**2.** Put the salmon on the prepared baking sheet and season it with salt and pepper. Bake in the oven until the flesh flakes easily with a fork, or to desired doneness, 6 to 8 minutes. Remove from the oven and drizzle with maple syrup.

**3.** Meanwhile, in a medium skillet, melt the butter over medium-high heat. Add the bell pepper and mushrooms and cook, stirring often, until softened, about 7 minutes. Drizzle the vegetables with vinegar and season with salt and pepper if necessary. Cook, stirring, for 30 seconds.

**4.** Divide the greens between 2 plates and top each portion with half of the bell pepper mixture. Place 1 piece of salmon on each portion of vegetables and serve immediately.

2 pieces boneless, skinless salmon (about 5 oz/140 g each)
Kosher salt and freshly ground black pepper to taste
1 tbsp (15 mL) pure maple syrup
2 tbsp (30 mL) unsalted butter
1 red bell pepper, seeded and chopped
2 portobello mushrooms, stems removed and caps chopped
1 tbsp (15 mL) balsamic vinegar
2 to 4 cups (500 mL to 1 L) mixed baby greens

## » CAJÚ'S BRAZILIAN FISH STEW

MAKES 4 SERVINGS

1-½ lb (680 g) boneless, skinless, firm, white-fleshed fish fillets (such as Pacific halibut, Pacific cod or black grouper), cut into 4 pieces and patted dry

Kosher salt to taste

2 tbsp (30 mL) fresh lime juice

2 tbsp (30 mL) extra virgin olive oil

½ cup (125 mL) finely chopped yellow onion

½ cup (125 mL) seeded and finely chopped green bell pepper

½ cup (125 mL) seeded and finely chopped yellow bell pepper

1 tbsp (15 mL) minced, peeled ginger

1 tsp (5 mL) minced garlic

1 tbsp (15 mL) tomato paste

1 cup (250 mL) canned diced tomatoes (undrained)

¾ cup (185 mL) chicken or fish broth

¾ cup (185 mL) well-stirred, canned unsweetened coconut milk

1 tsp (5 mL) hot sauce

2 tbsp (30 mL) chopped cilantro

Cooked white basmati rice for serving (optional)

At his restaurant Cajú (caju.ca), chef Mario Cassini show-cases contemporary Brazilian food, like this colourful fish stew (called moqueca) from northeastern Brazil. It has Native Indian and African influences and revolves around a tomato and coconut milk broth. Hot sauce gives it slight oomph, and cilantro makes it bright.

1. Season the fish with salt and rub all over with the lime juice. Marinate in the fridge while you prepare the sauce.

2. In a large skillet with a lid, heat the oil over medium heat. Add the onion, bell peppers, ginger and garlic, and cook, stirring often, until softened, about 7 minutes.

3. Stir in the tomato paste and cook for 1 minute. Add the tomatoes, with their juices, and the broth. Bring to a simmer and cook for 2 minutes.

4. Stir in the coconut milk and hot sauce, then add the fish. Bring to a simmer, then reduce the heat to medium-low. Simmer, covered, until the fish is cooked through, 5 to 10 minutes, depending on the thickness of the fish. Sprinkle with cilantro and serve alongside rice, if desired.

## » PICKEREL WITH MAPLE-CIDER SQUASH AND APPLES

MAKES 4 SERVINGS

4 skin-on pickerel fillets (each about 5 oz /140 g), rinsed and patted dry
Kosher salt and freshly ground black pepper to taste
¼ cup (60 mL) all-purpose flour
2 tbsp (30 mL) unsalted butter
1 tbsp (15 mL) vegetable oil
1 cup (250 mL) diced and peeled butternut squash (¼-inch/6 mm dice)
1 McIntosh apple (don't peel), cored and cut into ¼-inch (6 mm) dice
½ cup (125 mL) apple cider
2 tbsp (30 mL) pure maple syrup
Freshly squeezed lemon juice to taste

This patriotic pickerel comes from Rory Golden, the locally minded executive chef of Huntsville's Deerhurst Resort (deerhurstresort.com). If you can buy small pickerel fillets, use one per person. If not, use large fillets cut into portions.

**1.** Preheat the oven to 350°F (180°C). Season the pickerel with salt and pepper. Spread the flour out on a large plate and dredge each piece of pickerel in flour, shaking off the excess.

**2.** Heat a large, ovenproof skillet over medium-high heat. Add 1 tbsp (15 mL) butter and the oil, then add the pickerel, skin side up. Cook until the undersides are browned, 2 to 3 minutes.

**3.** Transfer the skillet to the oven and bake until the pickerel is cooked through and flakes easily with a fork, 6 to 8 minutes, depending on the thickness of the fish. Remove the pickerel to a large plate, cover loosely with foil and keep warm.

**4.** In the same skillet, and using an oven mitt to hold the handle if it's still hot, melt the remaining 1 tbsp (15 mL) butter over medium heat. Add the squash and cook, stirring often, for 4 minutes. Add the apple and cook, stirring, for 1 minute.

**5.** Add the cider and cook, stirring often, until the liquid reduces by about half and the squash is tender, about 4 minutes. Remove the skillet from the heat and stir in the maple syrup. Season to taste with lemon juice.

**6.** To serve, divide the pickerel among 4 plates or shallow bowls. Top each with the squash mixture, drizzling with any juices in the skillet.

David Friedman, chef and owner of Red Fish restaurant in Toronto, created this to showcase mackerel, a deliciously oily fish that gets the Ocean Wise seal of approval from the Vancouver Aquarium (oceanwise.ca) for being a sustainable seafood option. David favours bold, fruity, unpasteurized Izumi Nama-Nama from Ontario Spring Water Sake Co. (ontariosake.com) in the Distillery District, but you can use any brand from the liquor store.

I buy my fish at Hooked (hookedinc.ca) in Leslieville where they helpfully remove the pin bones and fins.

# RED MISO-BRAISED MACKEREL WITH RADISH

## MAKES 4 SERVINGS

4 skin-on mackerel fillets (each about 6 oz/170 g), skin lightly scored
1 lb (450 g) daikon or other Asian radishes, washed and peeled
½ cup (125 mL) peeled, julienned ginger
½ cup (125 mL) sake
½ cup (125 mL) water
2 tbsp (30 mL) red miso paste
1 tbsp (15 mL) granulated sugar
1 green onion, thinly sliced

**1.** Put the mackerel fillets, skin side up, in a colander set in the sink. Pour boiling water over the fillets to remove any fishy odour and clean the skin.

**2.** Cut the daikon radishes into very thin (¼-inch/6 mm) rounds, then halve or quarter the rounds if they're large.

**3.** Put the mackerel, daikon radishes, ginger, sake and water in a large skillet with a lid or a wide, shallow saucepan. Bring to a boil over high heat. Skim any scum from the surface, then reduce the heat to medium and cook, covered, for 5 minutes. Reduce the heat to low.

**4.** In a small bowl, whisk the miso with several tablespoonfuls of the cooking liquid until it dissolves. Stir in the sugar. Add the miso mixture to the skillet, gently stirring it around the fish if possible. Cook, covered, until the fish flakes easily with a fork, about 5 minutes.

**5.** To serve, carefully remove the mackerel to a cutting board. Cut each piece in half, if desired. Using a slotted spoon, divide the daikon radishes and ginger among 4 large, wide bowls. Top each with 1 large or 2 small pieces of mackerel, then pour the cooking liquid evenly over each portion. Garnish with the green onion.

# VEGETARIAN MAINS

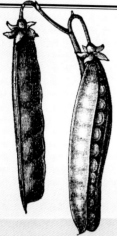

I'm an ardent carnivore who eats a lot of vegetarian meals, and not just because I have a vegetarian daughter, but because I find them to be creative and satisfying.

## » CARROT-QUINOA PIE

MAKES 6 SERVINGS

### Pastry

¾ cup (185 mL) whole wheat flour

¾ cup (185 mL) all-purpose flour

¼ cup (60 mL) vegetable oil

Pinch kosher salt

½ cup (125 mL) ice water, as needed

### Filling

2 cups (500 mL) grated, peeled carrots

1 medium yellow onion, finely diced

1 cup (250 mL) finely chopped flat-leaf parsley

1 cup (250 mL) grated cheddar-flavoured soy cheese

1 cup (250 mL) large-flake nutritional yeast

1 cup (250 mL) crumbled soft tofu

½ cup (125 mL) cooked quinoa

⅓ cup (80 mL) extra virgin olive oil

¼ cup (60 mL) tamari or soy sauce

3 large cloves garlic, minced

1 tsp (5 mL) dried marjoram

1 tsp (5 mL) dried basil leaves

¼ tsp (1 mL) cayenne

Freshly ground black pepper to taste

This intense, decadent vegetarian meal is one of my most treasured recipes. I got it in 2001 from Counter Culture, a student-owned-and-run restaurant that used to operate at York University. The key is nutritional yeast, which tastes cheesy and can be found at bulk and health food stores, and in the natural food area of some large supermarkets.

This pie is very flexible. Try millet instead of quinoa, raw carrots instead of steamed, or frozen pastry instead of fresh. You can even go crustless.

**1.** For the pastry, stir together the whole wheat and all-purpose flours in a medium bowl. Measure the oil into a small bowl. Put both bowls in the freezer for 1 hour until very cold.

**2.** Pour the oil into the flour mixture and, using a fork, mix until crumbly. Stir the salt into the ice water, then add ¼ cup (60 mL) of the water to the flour mixture. Mix with your hands, gradually adding more water, if necessary, until a smooth dough forms.

**3.** For a thick crust, roll out all the dough to an 11-inch (28 cm) round on a lightly floured surface. Lay the dough in a deep 9-inch (23 cm) pie plate, trim the edges and crimp.

**4.** For a thin crust, divide the dough in half, roll out 1 piece as above and freeze the other piece for future use.

**5.** For the filling, preheat the oven to 350°F (180°C). Steam the carrots over medium-high heat in a steamer insert in a medium saucepan, over 1 inch (2.5 cm) of simmering water, until tender, about 8 minutes.

**6.** In a medium bowl, combine the carrots, onion, parsley, soy cheese, nutritional yeast, tofu, quinoa, oil, tamari or soy sauce, garlic, marjoram, basil, cayenne and black pepper, and stir well.

**7.** Tip the filling into the prepared pie shell. Set the pie plate on a baking sheet (to catch any drips) and bake the pie in the centre of the oven until golden, about 40 minutes. Let the pie cool for 15 minutes before slicing.

## » MUJADDARA
### (RICE, LENTILS AND ONIONS)

MAKES 4 SERVINGS

3 cups (750 mL) water
1 cup (250 mL) dried green or
    brown lentils, rinsed
¾ cup (185 mL) long-grain
    brown rice, rinsed
1 tsp (5 mL) kosher salt
¼ cup (60 mL) vegetable oil
4 medium yellow onions, halved
    and thinly sliced
2 tsp (10 mL) ground cumin
1 tsp (5 mL) freshly ground
    black pepper
Plain yogurt for serving
    (optional)

Mujaddara, a peasant's dish of rice and lentils topped with cooked onions, is popular in the Middle East. I got this version from a Syrian cook at York University's Vegetarium Café, which has since closed, for a vegetarian recipe column I ran in 2001.

**1.** In a medium saucepan, combine the water, lentils, rice and salt and bring to a boil over high heat. Reduce the heat to low and simmer, covered, until the rice and lentils are tender and the water has been absorbed, about 45 minutes. Fluff with a fork.

**2.** Meanwhile, heat the oil in a large skillet over medium-high heat. Add the onions and cook, stirring often, until very brown, 30 to 40 minutes, reducing the heat if the onions start to char. Add the cumin and pepper and cook, stirring, for 2 minutes.

**3.** Divide the rice mixture among 4 bowls and top each portion with spiced onions. Top each with a dollop of yogurt (if using).

Japanese curry is thick and sweet and nothing like Indian curry. It's often served with white rice alongside breaded, fried chicken or pork cutlets (like the Tonkatsu on page 124). In Japan, people usually buy instant curry mixes in block or powder form. Asian and some mainstream supermarkets sell the block variety here. Popular brands include Glico, Vermont, Golden and Java, which come in various spice levels. I favour Glico since it's MSG free.

# JAPANESE CURRY «
# WITH VEGETABLES

MAKES 4 SERVINGS

2 tbsp (30 mL) vegetable oil
1 medium yellow onion,
    chopped
1 carrot, peeled and chopped
1 white potato, peeled, if
    desired, and chopped
2 large cloves garlic, minced
2 cups (500 mL) water, plus
    more if needed
1 package (110 g/3.8 oz) Japanese
    curry sauce mix, broken into
    pieces
Steamed rice for serving

**1.** In a medium saucepan, heat the oil over medium-high heat. Add the onion and cook, stirring often, for 3 minutes. Add the carrot, potato and garlic and cook, stirring often, for 4 minutes.

**2.** Add 2 cups (500 mL) water and bring to a boil. Reduce the heat to medium-low and cook, covered, stirring occasionally, until the vegetables are tender, about 20 minutes.

**3.** Add the curry sauce mix and cook, stirring often, until completely melted, about 5 minutes. Remove from the heat and let stand, covered, for 10 minutes. Stir well and, if desired, thin the curry with a little more water. Serve the curry alongside rice.

Shahan ful (pronounced "fool") is actually a breakfast dish but I eat it whenever the mood strikes. I got the recipe in 2001 from the now-defunct Selam Restaurant. Berbere is a distinctive Ethiopian blend of chilies, coriander, cardamom, fenugreek, garlic, ginger and other spices. Look for it in African grocery stores (see My Favourite Places to Shop, page 228).

# SPICY ETHIOPIAN ≪ FAVA BEANS

## (SHAHAN FUL)

MAKES 2 SERVINGS

1 tbsp (15 mL) vegetable oil
1 small yellow onion, minced
1 large clove garlic, minced
1-½ tsp (7 mL) berbere
    (Ethiopian spice blend)
½ tsp (2 mL) freshly ground
    black pepper
¼ tsp (1 mL) ground cumin
1 can (19 oz/540 mL) fava beans
    (ful medammas), undrained
1 tsp (5 mL) ghee (clarified
    butter; optional)
¼ cup (60 mL) plain yogurt
1 tomato, diced
1 jalapeño pepper or fresh green
    chili, with seeds, minced
2 crusty Italian rolls or other
    white buns (optional)

**1.** In a medium saucepan, heat the oil over medium heat. Add the onion and garlic and cook, stirring often, until softened, about 7 minutes. Add the berbere, black pepper and cumin and cook, stirring, for 1 minute.

**2.** Add the fava beans, with their juices, and cook, stirring often, for 10 minutes. Reduce the heat to low and cook, stirring constantly, until the mixture is very thick, about 5 minutes. If the fava beans don't break down, mash them with a wooden spoon. Stir in the ghee (if using), then remove from the heat.

**3.** Divide the fava bean mixture between 2 bowls. Top each with large dollop of yogurt, a pile of tomato and a pile of jalapeño or chilies. To eat, stir the toppings into the fava beans and eat with a roll (if using).

## » DAVE CARROLL'S SPICY CHANNA

MAKES 3–4 SERVINGS

2 tbsp (30 mL) vegetable oil
1 medium yellow onion, diced
3 large cloves garlic, minced
1 tbsp (15 mL) cumin seeds, or
    to taste
2 tsp (10 mL) ground cumin, or
    to taste
2 tsp (10 mL) garam masasla, or
    to taste
Pinch pure Indian chili powder
    or cayenne
1 can (14 oz/398 mL) diced
    tomatoes, undrained
1 can (19 oz/540 mL) chickpeas,
    drained and rinsed
Steamed brown or white
    basmati rice for serving
    (optional)

"I use this recipe all the time to the delight of my curry-mad family."

**LIBBY STEPHENS,** TORONTO

Dave Carroll is the manager of the FreshCo supermarket in Regent Park. When the store opened, he shared this recipe for aggressively spiced channa (chickpea curry), which he learned to make from his former mother-in-law, who is Indian. You might want to dial down the spices to start, then work your way up.

**1.** In a medium saucepan, heat the oil over medium heat. Add the onion and garlic and cook, stirring often, until softened, about 7 minutes.

**2.** Add the cumin seeds, ground cumin, garam masala and chili powder or cayenne, and cook, stirring often, for 3 minutes.

**3.** Add the tomatoes, with their juices, and bring to a simmer. Cook, stirring often, for 5 minutes. Stir in the chickpeas. Reduce the heat to low and cook, covered, stirring occasionally, to allow the flavours to develop, about 20 minutes. Serve the channa over rice (if using).

*Right: Ethiopian berbere*

## » JACKET POTATOES WITH BAKED BEANS AND CHEDDAR

MAKES 4 SERVINGS

4 small baking potatoes
  (preferably russets)
Fine sea salt or kosher salt to
  taste
Extra virgin olive oil to taste
1 can (14 oz/398 mL) baked
  beans
½ cup (125 mL) grated cheddar
  cheese
Unsalted butter to taste

There have been a couple of spots in Toronto that specialized in baked potatoes with a variety of toppings but, sadly, neither lasted. In the UK they call these "jacket potatoes" and are mad for them. Use whatever toppings you like, but consider this classic combo a starting point. I buy Amy's Organic or Eden Organic baked beans. Both are vegetarian.

**1.** Preheat the oven to 425°F (220°C). Wash the potatoes and dry them slightly with a clean towel. Sprinkle with salt and rub with oil. Put the potatoes directly on the centre rack of the oven and bake for 45 minutes.

**2.** Wearing oven mitts or using a thick towel, squeeze the potatoes. If the potatoes have crisp skins but give slightly when you press them, they're ready. If not, bake for 15 more minutes or until tender. Put each potato on a plate.

**3.** Meanwhile, heat the beans in a small saucepan over medium heat. Alternatively, microwave the beans on high power in a microwave-safe bowl covered with vented plastic wrap until heated through, about 3 minutes. Transfer the beans to a serving bowl. Put the cheese in a second serving bowl.

**4.** To eat, slice each potato down the centre, then gently press the ends toward the centre to open it up. Add butter to taste and mash the flesh well with a fork. Spoon some of the beans into the cavity and top with cheese.

Bala Thangarajah is a cook at the St. Joseph's Health Centre cafeteria, the Lakeview Café. He's from Sri Lanka and makes this popular curry once a week. People used to complain it was too hot—now they complain if it's not spicy enough. You may have to visit a Sri Lankan grocery store (like New Spiceland in Scarborough) for the spices, but I've given Indian alternatives that might be easier to find.

**1.** In a medium saucepan, heat the oil over medium-high heat. Add the onions, curry leaves and fennel seeds and cook, stirring often, until browned, about 6 minutes. Add the garlic and ginger and cook, stirring, for 2 minutes.

**2.** Add the tomatoes, with their juices, and the cilantro stems and bring to a boil. Reduce the heat to low and simmer, covered, for 10 minutes. Add the Jaffna curry powder or chili powder, and yellow curry powder and simmer for 5 minutes.

**3.** Using a handheld immersion blender in the saucepan (or in a blender or food processor), purée the tomato mixture until a smooth sauce forms.

**4.** Return the sauce to the saucepan if necessary. Add the chickpeas and ½ cup (125 mL) coconut milk. Increase the heat to medium and cook until heated through, about 3 minutes.

**5.** If the sauce seems too thick, add the remaining ½ cup (125 mL) coconut milk and heat through. Stir in the Sri Lankan "curry flavour" spice blend or garam masala. Sprinkle with cilantro leaves and serve with rice or naan (if using).

# SRI LANKAN CHICKPEA CURRY «

MAKES 4 SERVINGS

1 tbsp (15 mL) vegetable oil
2 medium yellow onions, minced in a mini food processor
5 fresh curry leaves
1 tsp (5 mL) fennel seeds
1 tsp (5 mL) minced garlic
1 tsp (5 mL) minced, peeled ginger
1-½ cups (375 mL) undrained, canned diced tomatoes
2 tbsp (30 mL) chopped cilantro stems
1 tbsp (15 mL) roasted hot Jaffna curry powder or 2 tsp (10 mL) pure chili powder (such as pequín or ancho)
1 tbsp (15 mL) yellow curry powder
1 can (19 oz/540 mL) chickpeas, drained and rinsed
½ to 1 cup (125 to 250 mL) well-stirred, canned unsweetened coconut milk, as needed
1 tsp (5 mL) Sri Lankan "curry flavour" spice blend or garam masala
2 tbsp (30 mL) chopped cilantro leaves
Steamed basmati rice or naan bread for serving (optional)

When you order a masala dosa at a South Indian restaurant, it will come with a scoop of spicy filling. This and the one on page 156 are my favourite dosa fillings at Udupi Palace (udupipalace.ca) in Gerrard India Bazaar. Thanks to freelance writer Smita Chandra for getting these two recipes for a story on dosas, and to restaurant owner Hubert D'Mello for sharing them. Serve with basmati rice or warmed naan or roti, or buy ready-made dosa batter at an Indian supermarket and make your own dosas following the instructions on the package.

## POTATO MASALA «

MAKES ABOUT 4 SERVINGS

1-½ lb (680 g) Yukon Gold or white potatoes, peeled and cut into small chunks

2 finger-length dried red chilies (preferably Kashmiri), broken into pieces

½ tsp (2 mL) black mustard seeds

¼ tsp (1 mL) cumin seeds

¼ tsp (1 mL) white urad dal (skinned, split urad lentils), rinsed

¼ tsp (1 mL) channa dal (yellow split peas), rinsed

3 tbsp (45 mL) vegetable oil

2 medium yellow onions, halved and thinly sliced

15 fresh curry leaves

2 small fresh green chilies, stems removed

1 tbsp (15 mL) minced, peeled ginger

½ tsp (2 mL) turmeric

Kosher salt to taste

2 tbsp (30 mL) chopped cilantro

**1.** In a medium saucepan of boiling water, simmer the potatoes until they're tender, 10 to 15 minutes. Drain well, then mash with a potato masher or a fork until smooth. Set aside.

**2.** In a small bowl, combine the dried red chilies, black mustard seeds, cumin seeds, urad dal and channa dal.

**3.** In a large non-stick skillet, heat the oil over medium-high heat. Add the dried red chili mixture and cook, stirring, for 30 seconds. Add the onions, curry leaves, green chilies and ginger, and cook, stirring often, until browned, 8 to 10 minutes, reducing the heat to medium if the vegetables start to scorch.

**4.** Add the turmeric and salt to taste and cook for 1 minute. Add the mashed potatoes, mixing well with a wooden spoon. Reduce the heat to medium-low and cook, stirring often, for 5 minutes until well blended. Stir in the cilantro. Transfer to a serving bowl.

*Left: Fresh curry leaves and turmeric*

## » PANEER MASALA

MAKES ABOUT 4 SERVINGS

2 tbsp (30 mL) vegetable oil
1 medium yellow onion, finely
    chopped
2 cloves garlic, minced
2 tsp (10 mL) minced, peeled
    ginger
1 tsp (5 mL) dried fenugreek
    leaves
½ tsp (2 mL) turmeric
½ tsp (2 mL) pure chili powder
    (such as pequín or ancho) or
    cayenne
¼ tsp (1 mL) fine sea salt
2 cups (500 mL) finely grated
    paneer (about 5 oz/140 g)
2 plum (roma) tomatoes, finely
    chopped
2 tbsp (30 mL) chopped cilantro

Another South Indian favourite from Udupi Palace and Hubert D'Mello via Smita Chandra. Paneer is a soft, white, fresh Indian cheese. Serve this with rice, Indian bread or dosas (look for ready-made dosa batter at an Indian supermarket).

**1.** In a large non-stick skillet, heat the oil over medium heat. Add the onion and cook, stirring often, for 5 minutes. Add the garlic and ginger and cook, stirring, for 1 minute.

**2.** Add the fenugreek, turmeric, chili or cayenne and salt. Cook, stirring, for 1 minute. Add the paneer and cook, stirring, for 2 minutes.

**3.** Gently stir in the tomatoes and cilantro and cook, stirring, for 1 minute. Transfer to a serving bowl.

These pancakes, which have a nice crust and a creamy interior, come from Venezuela and are served at Phil's Original BBQ (philsoriginalbbq.com) because owner Phil Nyman's wife, Gloria, is Venezuelan. If you can find it, panela (a fresh, white, cow's milk cheese) can be used instead of mozzarella. Depending on your skillet and stove, you'll have to play around with the heat here—it's somewhere between medium and medium-high. Serve these with a salad and you have a nice, light supper.

**1.** In a food processor or a blender, combine the corn kernels, eggs, flour, sugar and salt, then process until combined but still lumpy, 10 to 15 seconds. Don't overprocess to a liquid. Transfer the mixture to a bowl and use immediately or refrigerate, covered, for up to 1 day.

**2.** Heat a large cast iron skillet over medium heat, or a large non-stick skillet over medium-high heat. Swirl 1 tsp (5 mL) butter into the skillet, then quickly pour in ¾ cup (185 mL) corn batter.

**3.** Using a ladle or the back of a large spoon, lightly spread the batter in a circular motion to make a 6- to 7-inch (15 to 18 cm) pancake. Cook until the underside is lightly browned, bubbles form on the surface and the pancake is firm enough to flip, 3 to 4 minutes.

**4.** Carefully flip the pancake with a spatula. Spread ¼ cup (60 mL) cheese over half of the pancake. Cook until the cheese melts, the pancake is cooked through and the underside is browned, 3 to 4 minutes.

**5.** Transfer the pancake to a plate, then carefully fold the plain half over the melted cheese like an omelette (don't worry if it breaks slightly). Cover loosely with foil and keep warm. Repeat with the remaining butter, corn batter and cheese to make another 3 pancakes.

# CORN PANCAKES WITH CHEESE
## (CACHAPAS)

MAKES 4 SERVINGS

3-½ cups (875 mL) frozen corn kernels, thawed

3 large eggs

½ cup (125 mL) all-purpose flour

1 tbsp (15 mL) granulated sugar

½ tsp (2 mL) kosher salt

4 tsp (20 mL) unsalted butter for frying

1 cup (250 mL) coarsely grated mozzarella cheese

## » PORTOBELLO-QUINOA STACKS

MAKES 4 SERVINGS

2 cups (500 mL) water or
vegetable broth, plus more
water as needed
1 cup (250 mL) dried white or
red quinoa, rinsed
1 package (5 oz/142 g) baby
spinach
4 large portobello mushrooms,
stems removed
½ cup (125 mL) Habeeb's
Babaghanouj (page 38) or
My Favourite Hummus
(page 40) or use purchased
versions
2 tomatoes, seeded and diced
Hemp oil or fruity extra virgin
olive oil for drizzling

Inspired by a dish I enjoyed in a vegetarian restaurant in Calgary, I replicated this at home because it combines lots of my favourite flavours. Hemp oil is green and nutty, and available in the refrigerated section of health food stores or the natural food section of some large supermarkets.

If this artful stack seems too fussy, deconstruct the dish by scattering the quinoa over four plates and topping each pile with a portobello. Smear each mushroom with babaghanouj or hummus and top with spinach. Scatter the tomatoes over the plate and drizzle everything with oil.

**1.** In a medium saucepan, bring the water or broth and quinoa to a boil over high heat. Reduce the heat to low, then simmer, covered, until the water has been absorbed, 12 to 15 minutes. Fluff the quinoa with a fork, transfer to a bowl and keep warm.

**2.** In the same saucepan, bring 1 inch (2.5 cm) water to a boil over high heat. Add the spinach and cook, covered, just until the spinach wilts, 1 to 2 minutes. Drain the spinach well. Transfer the spinach to a fine-mesh sieve and press out any remaining liquid with a wooden spoon. Tip the spinach into a second bowl and keep warm.

**3.** Meanwhile, put the portobello caps, gill sides down, on a rimmed baking sheet. Broil under high heat until tender, about 4 minutes per side.

**4.** To assemble the stacks, put 1 mushroom cap, gill side up, on each of 4 plates. Spread each mushroom cap with 2 tbsp (30 mL) babaghanouj or hummus, then top with the quinoa. Spoon one-quarter of the spinach on top of the quinoa (spoon each portion of spinach into a measuring cup or small bowl to help form it). Top each stack with tomatoes and drizzle with oil.

## » SALVADORAN PUPUSAS WITH FRESH SLAW

MAKES 8 SERVINGS

**Fresh Slaw**

2 cups (500 mL) shredded
    green cabbage
1 carrot, peeled and grated
1-½ cups (375 mL) white vinegar
1 finger-length fresh red chili,
    seeded, if desired, and
    minced, or dried red chili
    flakes (optional)
1 tsp (5 mL) granulated sugar
½ tsp (2 mL) dried oregano

**Salvadoran Pupusas**

2 cups (500 mL) instant yellow
    corn masa flour (such as
    Maseca brand)
1-¼ cups (310 mL) warm water,
    plus more if needed
¼ tsp (1 mL) kosher salt
Vegetable oil for greasing and
    frying
½ cup (125 mL) grated
    mozzarella or crumbled
    queso fresco (or other fresh
    Spanish cheese) and/or
    refried beans
All-Purpose Tomato Sauce
    (page 181) or purchased
    tomato sauce, at room
    temperature

One of the first things I did on the food beat in 2001 was go to a Salvadoran restaurant for a tutorial on how to make pupusas, the thick, corn flour pancakes that are usually stuffed with pork, cheese, beans and other fillings. With cheese and/or beans, and served with a simple, vinegary slaw (curtido) and your favourite tomato sauce, pupusas make a great vegetarian main dish.

**1.** For the Fresh Slaw, toss together the cabbage and carrot in a medium bowl. In a small bowl, stir together the vinegar, fresh chili or dried chili flakes (if using), sugar and oregano. Pour the vinegar mixture over the cabbage mixture and stir well. Cover and refrigerate for at least 1 hour.

**2.** For the Salvadoran Pupusas, combine the masa, 1-¼ cups (310 mL) water and the salt in a medium bowl. Use your hands to mix the ingredients to a dough. Knead the dough in the bowl until smooth, about 2 minutes. Let stand, covered with a damp cloth, for 10 minutes.

**3.** Divide the dough into 8 balls and, with well-oiled hands, pat each ball into a 3-inch (7.5 cm) disc between your palms. Fill the centre of 1 disc with 1 tbsp (15 mL) cheese or beans (or a mixture). Cup the filled disc in 1 hand and ease the dough up around the filling, pinching the edges of the dough together to seal in the filling and create the pupusa.

**4.** Add more oil to your hands and, slapping the pupusa between your palms, pat it into a 5-inch (13 cm) disc. Alternatively, put the pupusa on a cutting board and pat it into shape. Set the pupusa aside on a large plate and repeat with the remaining discs of dough, cheese and/or beans.

**5.** In a large non-stick skillet, heat about 1 tbsp (15 mL) oil over medium heat. Cook the pupusas, in batches, until golden and blistered in spots, for about 6 minutes per side, pressing down on the pupusas every 2 minutes with a metal spatula. Add more oil to the skillet before cooking each batch.

**6.** When ready to serve, use a slotted spoon to remove the Fresh Slaw from its liquid. Drizzle the pupusas with room-temperature Tomato Sauce and serve with the Fresh Slaw.

Jean's Vegetarian Kitchen is a Thai restaurant run by Harry and Jean Seow where everything's made from scratch. He's from Malaysia, she's from Thailand and they're both Chinese so their food shows many influences. Serve this mildly spicy tofu with cooked white rice or coconut rice. Freeze the extra ginger-chili sauce for when you make this dish again. Or stir the extra sauce into a stir-fry, rice or noodle dish.

# GINGER-CHILI TOFU

«

MAKES 4 SERVINGS

**Ginger-Chili Sauce**
5 small dried red chilies (each 1 to 2 inches/2.5 to 5 cm)
¼ cup (60 mL) thinly sliced shallots
2 tbsp (30 mL) minced garlic
2 tbsp (30 mL) chopped, peeled ginger
2 tsp (10 mL) vegetable oil

**Tofu**
1 lb (450 g) firm tofu, cut into 24 bite-size triangles
2 tbsp (30 mL) vegetable oil
1 carrot, peeled and cut into very thin rounds
¼ cup (60 mL) vegetable broth or water
3 tbsp (45 mL) white vinegar
1-½ tbsp (22 mL) granulated sugar
1 tbsp (15 mL) ketchup
1 tsp (5 mL) soy sauce
Kosher salt and freshly ground white or black pepper to taste

**1.** For the Ginger-Chili Sauce, put the dried red chilies in a small bowl and add enough very hot water just to cover them. Soak for 1 hour or until softened.

**2.** Discard any stems and transfer the chilies, with their soaking liquid, to a mini food processor, along with the shallots, garlic and ginger. Process until smooth.

**3.** In a small skillet or saucepan, heat the oil over medium-high heat. Add the chili paste and reduce the heat to medium-low. Cook, stirring often, for 12 minutes.

**4.** Spoon out 1 tbsp (15 mL) of the Ginger-Chili Sauce to use for this recipe. Refrigerate the remaining sauce (or freeze in 1 tbsp/15 mL portions) for future use.

**5.** For the tofu, lay the pieces out in a single layer on a large paper-towel-lined plate for at least 30 minutes to drain.

**6.** In a large non-stick skillet, heat the oil over medium-high heat. Add the tofu in a single layer and cook until browned on both sides, flipping once, about 2 minutes per side.

**7.** In a medium bowl, combine the reserved 1 tbsp (15 mL) Ginger-Chili Sauce, the carrot, broth or water, vinegar, sugar, ketchup and soy sauce. Add to the tofu in the skillet and cook, stirring gently or shaking the skillet, until the sauce is syrupy and the tofu is coated, 1 to 2 minutes. Season with salt and pepper if necessary.

# NOODLES AND PASTA

I have a weakness for Chinese noodles and am still learning the best way to eat each kind. My wok is a treasured friend, but I can't pass up Italian pasta either. Who can?

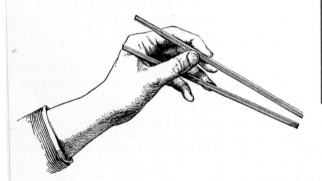

*Left: (clockwise from top left) Miki, chow mein, e-fu and Shanghai noodles*

## » CHINESE FOOD TRUCK NOODLES

MAKES 4–6 SERVINGS

3 tbsp (45 mL) peanut or
vegetable oil
2 tbsp (30 mL) minced garlic
1 tbsp (15 mL) peeled, minced
ginger
1 lb (450 g) ground pork
3 green onions, thinly sliced
8 to 12 oz (225 to 340 g) firm or
extra-firm tofu, cut into small
cubes
¼ cup (60 mL) ground bean
sauce
1 tbsp (15 mL) Asian chili oil
or 2 tsp (10 mL) Sriracha or
other Asian hot sauce
2 tsp (10 mL) granulated sugar
1-½ tsp (7 mL) sesame oil
½ tsp (2 mL) freshly ground
black pepper
1 lb (450 g) fresh, thick, round
Chinese wheat noodles (such
as white Shanghai)

Toronto's street food scene is finally moving beyond hot dogs thanks to intrepid food truckers and creative street vendors. Still, we often look to America for inspiration. I adore these fiery noodles, adapted from a recipe in Chicago journalist Heather Shouse's book *Food Trucks: Dispatches from the Best Kitchens on Wheels* (Ten Speed Press, 2011). She created it by watching the Yue Kee truck owners in Philadelphia at work.

Ground bean sauce, made from naturally fermented soybeans, is the secret ingredient (I prefer the Lee Kum Kee brand). It provides umami (or rich savouriness), the fifth taste after sweet, sour, salty and bitter.

**1.** In a large wok or skillet, heat 2 tbsp (30 mL) peanut or vegetable oil over high heat for 1 minute. Add the garlic and ginger, and cook, stirring, for 2 minutes. Add the pork and green onions, and stir-fry, breaking up the meat with a wooden spoon, until the pork is cooked through and lightly browned, about 5 minutes.

**2.** Add the tofu, bean sauce, chili oil or hot sauce, and sugar, and stir-fry for 2 minutes. Remove the wok from the heat and stir in the sesame oil and pepper. Cover and keep warm.

**3.** Meanwhile, bring a large pot of water to a boil over high heat. Add the noodles, then cook according to the package instructions, 2 to 5 minutes. Drain the noodles, then toss them with the remaining 1 tbsp (15 mL) peanut or vegetable oil so they don't clump.

**4.** Divide the noodles among 4 or 6 large bowls or plates. Top with the stir-fried pork and tofu, dividing evenly. Eat the noodles with chopsticks, mixing the noodles and pork and tofu as you go.

## » STIR-FRIED NOODLES WITH BEAN SPROUTS

MAKES 4 SERVINGS

1 tbsp (15 mL) water
1 tsp (15 mL) mushroom-
   flavoured dark soy sauce
2 tbsp (30 mL) vegetable oil
8 oz (225 g) Cantonese-style,
   steamed chow mein noodles
   (about 4 cups/1 L)
3 tbsp (45 mL) light soy sauce
4 cups (1 L) bean sprouts
   (preferably mung bean),
   washed
10 thin, 2-inch (5 cm) long slices
   seeded green bell pepper

I couldn't get these deceptively simple noodles to taste right until Simon Peng, the owner of Simon's Wok Vegetarian Kitchen, showed me that less is more and mushroom-flavoured soy sauce is key. Simon, who is from Shenzhen, China, favours Pearl River Bridge brand soy sauces.

Look for fresh chow mein noodles in the refrigerated noodle area of Asian supermarkets. If you don't like bell peppers, use onions or green onions instead. Health Canada advises we fully cook our sprouts, so if you're feeding kids, seniors or anyone with a compromised immune system, cook the vegetable mixture for an extra minute.

**1.** In a small bowl, combine the water and mushroom-flavoured soy sauce. Set aside.

**2.** Heat a large wok or skillet over high heat, then add the oil, swirling it around the wok or skillet until well coated. Add the noodles and stir-fry, tossing and stirring constantly with a wok spatula, for 30 seconds.

**3.** Drizzle the noodles with light soy sauce and stir-fry for 2 minutes. Add the bean sprouts, bell pepper and mushroom soy mixture, and stir-fry for 1 minute. Transfer the noodles to a serving platter and serve immediately.

"I live in North Bay but travel to Toronto many times a year just to dine. Vegetarian Haven was one of my most memorable food discoveries. I still dream of their Vegan Shanghai Noodles, a perfect balance of soft slurpability, crispy texture, and subtly sweet, savoury flavours."

**JOSÉE GUILLEMETTE,** NORTH BAY, ONT.

This vegan dish comes from chef Jack Li at Vegetarian Haven (vegetarianhaven.com), restaurateur Shing Tong's popular Asian-style restaurant. Use whatever noodle you like. My favourites are Shanghai (a.k.a. miki) noodles, which come pre-cooked (check the label), or ready-cooked Japanese udon noodles, which are now in supermarkets in shelf-stable packages.

**1.** In a small bowl, whisk together the water, soy sauce, hoisin sauce, vegetarian "oyster" or stir-fry sauce, vinegar and sugar. Set aside.

**2.** In the wok or a large skillet, heat the vegetable oil over high heat. Add the ginger, and stir-fry for 20 seconds. Add the carrot and mushrooms, and stir-fry for 2 minutes. Add the tofu, celery, zucchini and bell pepper, and stir-fry for 2 minutes.

**3.** Reduce the heat to medium-high, and add the noodles, bean sprouts and soy sauce mixture. Stir-fry until the noodles are softened, the sprouts are cooked and the sauce is syrupy, about 2 minutes. Transfer the noodles to a serving platter. Drizzle with the sesame oil, sprinkle with the sesame seeds and serve immediately.

# SHANGHAI NOODLES «

**READERS' CHOICE**

MAKES 2–3 SERVINGS

½ cup (125 mL) water
2 tbsp (30 mL) soy sauce
2 tbsp (30 mL) hoisin sauce
1 tbsp (15 mL) vegetarian "oyster" or vegetarian mushroom-flavoured stir-fry sauce
1 tsp (5 mL) rice vinegar
1 tsp (5 mL) granulated sugar
1 tbsp (15 mL) vegetable oil
2 tsp (10 mL) minced, peeled ginger
1 carrot, peeled and sliced into thin rounds
4 white or brown mushrooms, sliced
4 oz (115 g) firm tofu, cut into thin strips
1 stalk celery, cut into thin strips
½ small zucchini, halved and thinly sliced
½ red bell pepper, seeded and cut into thin strips
14 oz (400 g) pre-cooked, yellow Shanghai (miki) noodles, rinsed and separated under hot water
1 cup (250 mL) bean sprouts (preferably mung bean), washed
1 tsp (5 mL) sesame oil
1 tsp (5 mL) toasted sesame seeds

## » CURRIED NOODLES WITH TOFU AND VEGGIES

### (MEE GORENG)

MAKES 4 SERVINGS

1 lb (450 g) fresh white Shanghai noodles or other thin flour noodles
3 tbsp (45 mL) vegetable oil
1 large egg
2 tbsp (30 mL) minced yellow onion
1 tsp (5 mL) minced garlic
2 cups (500 mL) mixed, bite-size pieces firm tofu and vegetables (see introduction)
1 tbsp (15 mL) curry paste
1 cup (250 mL) bean sprouts (preferably mung bean), washed
1 tomato, diced
3 tbsp (45 mL) ketchup
1 green onion, finely chopped
1 tsp (5 mL) granulated sugar
1 tsp (5 mL) kosher salt
¼ tsp (1 mL) freshly ground white or black pepper
Splash soy sauce

Harry Seow includes some of his native Malaysian dishes at Jean's Vegetarian Kitchen, the Thai restaurant he runs with his wife, Jean. Harry makes and sells his own curry paste, but you can use any brand. White Shanghai noodles are in the refrigerated section of Asian supermarkets. For the vegetables, choose a mix of broccoli or cauliflower florets, sugar snap peas and/or trimmed snow peas.

**1.** In a large wok or saucepan filled with boiling water, cook the noodles over high heat according to the package instructions, 2 to 5 minutes. Drain in a colander, then rinse under cold water. Set aside.

**2.** In the wok or a large skillet, heat the oil to medium-high heat. Add the egg, yellow onion and garlic, and cook, stirring, for 1 minute. Add the tofu and vegetables, and cook, stirring, until tender-crisp, about 3 minutes.

**3.** Stir in the cooked noodles and the curry paste. Cook, tossing with tongs, for 1 minute or until well mixed.

**4.** Add the bean sprouts, tomato, ketchup, green onion, sugar, salt, pepper and soy sauce. Cook, stirring or tossing with tongs, until the ingredients are well mixed and heated through, 1 to 2 minutes. Transfer the noodles to a serving platter and serve immediately.

Purists go nuts when they see ketchup in a pad Thai recipe, but I learned this version (complete with ketchup) from a cooking school in Chiang Mai, Thailand, in 1995. I buy small tubs of tamarind concentrate (sometimes labelled sauce) from Asian supermarkets. If you can't find it, buy a block of preserved tamarind, break off ¼ cup (60 mL) of pieces, combine them with ⅓ cup (80 mL) boiling water, let stand for 15 minutes, then strain, discarding any seeds or solids. Rice sticks can be thick or thin. I prefer the ones that are almost the size of fettuccine.

**1.** In a large bowl, soak the noodles in enough hot tap water to cover them for 30 minutes. Drain well and rinse with cold water.

**2.** In a small bowl, whisk together the tamarind concentrate or sauce, ketchup, lime juice, soy or fish sauce, sugar and chili sauce.

**3.** In a large wok or skillet, heat the oil over medium-high heat. Add the tofu and garlic and stir-fry for 2 minutes. Increase the heat to high. Add the eggs and stir-fry until they are scrambled, 30 to 60 seconds.

**4.** Add the drained noodles, bean sprouts and tamarind mixture. Stir-fry, using tongs to lift and mix the noodles, until all the ingredients are heated through and well combined, 3 to 5 minutes.

**5.** Transfer the noodles to a serving platter and garnish with cilantro, peanuts, and green onions. Alternatively, add the cilantro, peanuts and green onions to the wok and toss well. Divide the noodles among 4 or 6 plates and pass the lime wedges separately.

# PAD THAI

MAKES 4 SERVINGS

½ lb (225 g) dried rice stick/vermicelli noodles (pad Thai or banh pho noodles)
¼ cup (60 mL) tamarind concentrate or sauce
¼ cup (60 mL) ketchup
Juice of 2 limes
3 tbsp (45 mL) light soy sauce or fish sauce
1 tbsp (15 mL) granulated sugar
1 tbsp (15 mL) Asian chili sauce (sambal oelek) or chili-garlic sauce
¼ cup (60 mL) vegetable oil
½ lb (225 g) firm or extra-firm tofu, cut in ½-inch (1 cm) cubes
5 cloves garlic, minced
4 large eggs, beaten
3 to 4 cups (750 mL to 1 L) bean sprouts (preferably mung bean), washed

**Garnish**
½ cup (125 mL) chopped cilantro
½ cup (125 mL) roasted, unsalted peanuts, coarsely chopped or finely crushed
5 green onions, cut in 1-inch (2.5 cm) pieces
Lime wedges

E-fu (sometimes labelled yi-mein or fried noodles) are egg noodles that have been dried, fried and packaged. Look for them in the refrigerated area of Asian supermarkets. Toronto chef Winlai Wong of Spice Route Asian Bistro & Bar (spiceroute.ca) made this chewy, nourishing dish for a FoodShare Toronto fundraiser called Recipe for Change in 2011.

# BRAISED E-FU NOODLES WITH KING OYSTER MUSHROOMS

## MAKES 4 SERVINGS

1 carrot, peeled and julienned
1 package (7 oz/200 g) "fried noodles" (e-fu noodles)
3 tbsp (45 mL) canola oil
1 cup (250 mL) vegetable broth
1 tbsp (15 mL) vegetarian "oyster" sauce or vegetarian mushroom-flavoured stir-fry sauce
1 tbsp (15 mL) soy sauce
1 tsp (5 mL) granulated sugar
4 king oyster mushrooms, trimmed and julienned
1 tbsp (15 mL) Shaoxing rice cooking wine
8 oz (225 g) snow peas, trimmed
1 tsp (5 mL) mushroom-flavoured dark soy sauce
1 tsp (5 mL) sesame oil

1. In a large wok or pot of boiling water, cook the carrot for 30 seconds. Using a slotted spoon, remove the carrot to a bowl.

2. Add the noodles to the water and cook for 1 minute, stirring and pushing the noodles under the water with a wooden spoon. Drain well. Lay the noodles out on a large baking sheet to prevent them clumping and breaking. Drizzle with 1 tbsp (15 mL) canola oil.

3. In a small bowl, stir together the broth, vegetarian "oyster" or stir-fry sauce, regular soy sauce and sugar. Set aside.

4. Heat the wok or a large non-stick skillet over medium-high heat, and add the remaining 2 tbsp (30 mL) canola oil. Add the mushrooms, and cook, stirring, for 2 minutes. Add the cooking wine, and cook, stirring, for 30 seconds.

5. Add the cooked noodles and the broth mixture to the wok, tossing with tongs until the noodles are well coated with the sauce.

6. Add the carrot and snow peas, and stir-fry for 1 minute. Stir in the mushroom soy sauce and sesame oil, and toss well. Transfer the noodles to a serving platter and serve immediately.

## » BUCATINI WITH SAUSAGE AND PEAS

Ⓡ Ⓔ Ⓐ Ⓓ Ⓔ Ⓡ Ⓢ '
Ⓒ Ⓗ Ⓞ Ⓘ Ⓒ Ⓔ

MAKES 4–6 SERVINGS

1 tbsp (15 mL) extra virgin olive oil
12 oz (340 g) spicy pork sausage (such as Italian, Mexican or Spanish), casings removed
1 small yellow onion, minced
3 large cloves garlic, minced
3 cups (750 mL) tomato sauce
1 cup (250 mL) frozen peas
¼ cup (60 mL) whipping cream
1 lb (450 g) dried bucatini
Freshly ground black pepper to taste
Freshly grated Parmigiano Reggiano cheese for serving

"This has become my signature dish, and a favourite of my kids and husband. I've made it for dinner parties and received wows all around. This is my go-to dish when I want to impress."

**NANCY RUSCICA,** TORONTO

Oddly, I have Sting to thank for my belated introduction to bucatini, a thick spaghetti-like pasta with a hole in the middle. I read in *Food & Wine* in 2007 about how the musician's private chef, Joe Sponzo, makes him a dish like this with wild boar sausage and garden peas, and over the years I've adapted the recipe.

**1.** In a large saucepan, heat the oil over medium-high heat. Add the sausage, and cook, breaking up the meat into small pieces with a wooden spoon, until lightly browned, 6 to 8 minutes. Add the onion and garlic, and cook, stirring, for about 3 minutes.

**2.** Add the tomato sauce and bring to a boil. Reduce the heat to low and simmer, covered and stirring occasionally, for 30 minutes. Stir in the peas and cream, and simmer, uncovered, for 10 minutes.

**3.** Meanwhile, in a large pot of boiling, salted water, cook the pasta according to the package instructions until al dente. Drain the pasta well and return it to the pot.

**4.** Add the sausage-tomato mixture to the pot and toss with tongs over low heat until the pasta is well coated with the sauce. Season with pepper to taste. Divide the pasta among 4 or 6 shallow bowls and pass the cheese separately.

## » TERRONI'S SPAGHETTI WITH ANCHOVIES AND BREAD CRUMBS

MAKES 4 SERVINGS

12 oz (340 g) dried spaghetti
¼ cup (60 mL) extra virgin olive oil
¼ cup (60 mL) dried bread crumbs
1 can (50 g) anchovy fillets packed in oil, drained and chopped
24 cherry tomatoes
20 pitted kalamata or other black olives
3 cloves garlic, minced
1 tbsp (15 mL) drained and rinsed capers
¼ tsp (1 mL) dried red chili flakes
2 tbsp (30 mL) finely chopped flat-leaf parsley

Restaurant critic Amy Pataki wrangled this recipe from Terroni executive chef Giovanna Alonzi in 2007. The restaurant (terroni.com) used Moroccan olives and handmade pasta, but Amy made things easier for home cooks. Don't be tempted to add cheese. The bread crumbs are there instead.

**1.** In a large pot of boiling, salted water, cook the spaghetti for 1 minute less than the package instructs. Remove ½ cup (125 mL) cooking water and set aside. Drain the pasta well.

**2.** Meanwhile, heat 1 tbsp (15 mL) oil in a large non-stick skillet over medium heat. Add the bread crumbs, and cook, stirring, until browned and toasted, 2 to 3 minutes. Transfer the bread crumbs to a small bowl.

**3.** Add the remaining 3 tbsp (45 mL) oil and the anchovies to skillet. Cook over medium heat, mashing the anchovies with a wooden spoon until they dissolve into the oil, about 2 minutes.

**4.** Add the tomatoes, olives, garlic, capers and chili flakes to the skillet, and cook, stirring, for 1 minute. Increase the heat to medium-high, and add the pasta and the reserved cooking water. Cook, tossing the pasta with tongs, until it is al dente and the liquid has been absorbed.

**5.** Using tongs, divide the pasta among 4 shallow bowls. Top each with the tomato-olive mixture, dividing evenly. Sprinkle each portion with the reserved bread crumbs, then the parsley.

"Now that my boys are young adults, they really enjoy this pasta with kale, chickpeas and Parmesan. I serve the cheese on the side as my younger son is vegan, and won't eat any animal products."

**MARY GRACE FONG,** AURORA, ONT.

A Toronto company called Cookin' Greens (cookingreens.com) sells convenient bags of frozen, chopped leafy vegetables such as kale. You can reach into the bag and grab a handful as needed. This pasta is adapted from one of the company's recipes. If you prefer, use another short pasta such as rotini or macaroni.

**1.** In a large saucepan of boiling, salted water, cook the pasta according to the package instructions until al dente. Drain well.

**2.** Meanwhile, heat the oil in a large non-stick skillet over medium-high heat. Add the onion and cook, stirring often, for 3 minutes. Add the garlic and cook, stirring, for 30 seconds.

**3.** Add the kale, chickpeas and sun-dried tomatoes and cook, stirring often, until heated through, about 5 minutes.

**4.** Stir in the drained pasta and ½ cup (125 mL) Parmigiano Reggiano and cook, stirring, until heated through. Season to taste with salt, pepper and chili flakes and serve sprinkled with more Parmigiano Reggiano if desired.

# FUSILLI WITH KALE AND CHICKPEAS

**READERS' CHOICE**

MAKES 4 SERVINGS

½ lb (225 g) dried fusilli (about 2-½ cups/625 mL)

2 tbsp (30 mL) extra virgin olive oil

1 medium yellow onion, halved and thinly sliced

2 large cloves garlic, minced

3 cups (750 mL) chopped frozen or fresh kale

1 can (19 oz/540 mL) chickpeas, drained and rinsed

⅓ cup (80 mL) drained and julienned sun-dried tomatoes packed in oil

½ cup (125 mL) freshly grated Parmigiano Reggiano, plus more for sprinkling

Kosher salt and freshly ground black pepper to taste

Dried red chili flakes to taste

Craig Harding, the chef-owner of Campagnolo restaurant (campagnolotoronto.com), made this classic Italian pasta for me, his mom and his nonna for a Mother's Day story. He uses handmade spaghetti but any dried pasta shape will do. Guanciale (gwan-cha-lay) is cured pork cheek (jowls), while pancetta is cured pork belly. Of the two, guanciale has the stronger flavour and is often seasoned with black pepper.

**1.** In a large pot of boiling, salted water, cook the pasta according to the package instructions until al dente. Drain well.

**2.** Meanwhile, in a large skillet, cook the guanciale or pancetta over medium heat until it is crispy and its fat is rendered, about 8 minutes. Add the garlic and chili flakes, and cook, stirring, for 1 minute. Add the Tomato Sauce, and cook, stirring, until heated through, about 2 minutes.

**3.** Add the drained pasta and 2 tbsp (30 mL) parsley, and toss well with tongs until the pasta is well coated with the sauce, 1 to 2 minutes.

**4.** Divide the pasta among 4 or 6 shallow bowls. Top each serving with some cheese, then sprinkle with the remaining 2 tbsp (30 mL) parsley.

# PASTA ALL'AMATRICIANA 《

MAKES 4–6 SERVINGS

1 lb (450 g) dried pasta (bucatini, spaghetti or your favourite shape)
4 oz (115 g) guanciale or pancetta, finely diced or cut into 1-inch (2.5 cm) slivers
2 large cloves garlic, very thinly sliced
¼ to ½ tsp (1 to 2 mL) dried red chili flakes, to taste
2 cups (500 mL) All-Purpose Tomato Sauce (page 181) or purchased tomato sauce
¼ cup (60 mL) chopped flat-leaf parsley
Finely grated Pecorino Romano cheese for serving

## » PASTA WITH TOMATO-BASIL SAUCE

MAKES 4 SERVINGS

**Basil-Garlic Oil**
¼ cup (60 mL) extra virgin olive oil
6 cloves garlic, peeled and smashed
8 large basil leaves
Pinch dried red chili flakes

**Tomato Sauce**
1 can (28 oz/796 mL) whole peeled tomatoes (preferably San Marzano), seeded if desired
Kosher salt and freshly ground black pepper to taste

**Pasta**
12 oz (340 g) dried pasta
2 tbsp (30 mL) unsalted butter
16 large basil leaves, thinly sliced crosswise
Freshly grated Parmigiano Reggiano cheese for serving

Inspired by chef Scott Conant's famously simple spaghetti dish at Scarpetta (a New York restaurant with a Toronto outpost), I cobbled together a streamlined recipe from Internet sources in 2010 and it has become my go-to pasta sauce. The recipe makes 3 cups (750 mL) sauce and it works well with all kinds of pasta, and as a base for other recipes, too.

**1.** For the Basil-Garlic Oil, heat the oil, garlic, basil and chili flakes in a small saucepan over low heat, until the garlic is golden, about 30 minutes. Strain the oil, reserving the solids for another use. (I eat the garlic and basil on toast or in sandwiches.)

**2.** For the Tomato Sauce, cook the tomatoes, with their juices, in a medium saucepan over medium heat, mashing the tomatoes with a potato masher and stirring occasionally, until the sauce thickens, about 30 minutes. Remove the saucepan from the heat and stir in the Basil-Garlic Oil. Taste and season with salt and pepper if necessary. (The sauce can be refrigerated in an airtight container for up to 5 days.)

**3.** For the pasta, cook it in a large pot of boiling, salted water for 1 minute less than the package instructs. Remove ½ cup (125 mL) cooking liquid and set aside. Drain the pasta well.

**4.** In a large non-stick skillet, heat the Tomato-Basil Garlic Sauce over medium-high heat until bubbling. Add the pasta and the reserved cooking liquid, and toss well with tongs, lifting the pasta and dropping it back into the pan until the pasta is just al dente and well coated with the sauce, 1 to 2 minutes.

**5.** Remove the skillet from the heat and add the butter and basil. Toss until the ingredients are well combined and the butter melts. Using tongs, divide the pasta among 4 shallow bowls. Drizzle any remaining sauce from the skillet over each portion and sprinkle with cheese.

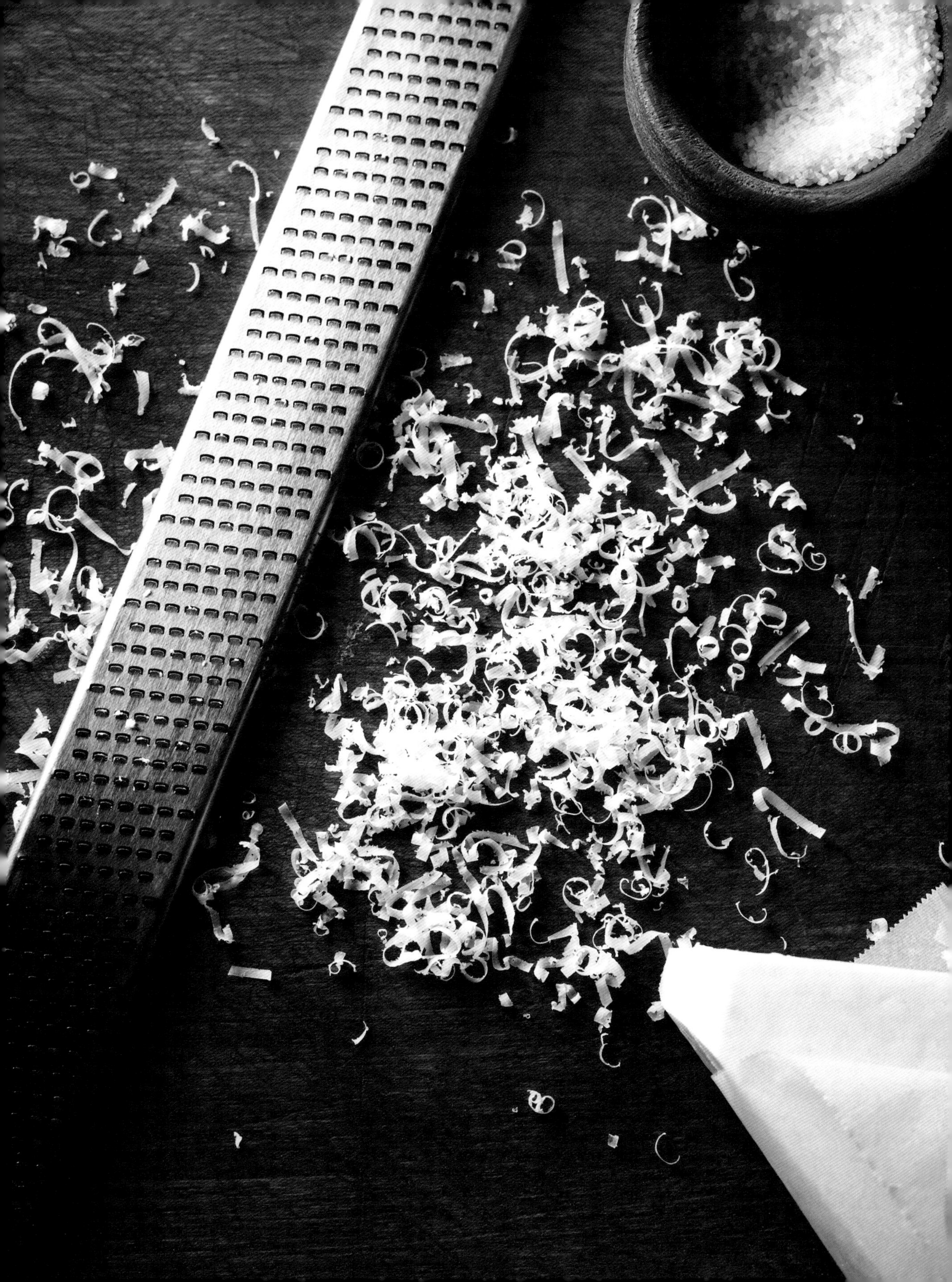

## » SPAGHETTI WITH BROWNED BUTTER AND MIZITHRA CHEESE

MAKES 4–6 SERVINGS

½ cup (125 mL) unsalted butter, cut into pieces
1 lb (450 g) dried spaghetti
¾ cup (185 mL) finely grated aged mizithra cheese (about 3-½ oz/100 g)

This is inspired by one of the signature dishes at The Old Spaghetti Factory (oldspaghettifactory.ca). The Toronto branch, on the Esplanade, has been a fixture here since 1971 and we've taken several stabs at the recipe, adding things like Romano, garlic and parsley. Finally, company president Peter Buckley gave me the proportions for the three-ingredient dish.

Aged mizithra (sometimes spelled myzithra) is a hard, salty, white Greek sheep's cheese, but you can use Italian ricotta salata, too. Ask your cheesemonger to finely grate it for you.

**1.** In a small saucepan, melt the butter over medium heat, watching closely and gently swirling the saucepan. The butter will foam and solids will start to separate out and turn brown after about 7 to 9 minutes. When it is golden and smells nutty, pour the melted browned butter into a small bowl to halt the cooking. (If there are any black flecks in the butter, strain them out.)

**2.** Meanwhile, in a large pot of boiling, salted water, cook the pasta according to the package instructions until it is al dente. Drain well and put it in a large bowl.

**3.** Drizzle the pasta with the browned butter and toss well with tongs. Sprinkle with ½ cup (125 mL) cheese, and toss well again.

**4.** Divide the pasta among 4 or 6 shallow bowls and sprinkle with the remaining ¼ cup (60 mL) cheese, dividing it evenly.

San Marzano is a variety of plum tomato named for the region in Italy near Naples where it's grown on volcanic soil. Chefs and foodies love the tart flavour, firm pulp and low seed count of San Marzanos, so it's no wonder the tomatoes have been given Protected Designation of Origin status by the European Union. Toss freelance writer Eric Vellend's sauce with your favourite pasta, or use it for his Margherita Pizza Bagels (page 63). "Tomato sauce freezes like a charm, so it's silly not to make at least a can's worth," says Eric.

**1.** In a medium saucepan, heat the oil over medium heat. Add the garlic and cook, stirring, for 2 minutes or until softened but not brown.

**2.** Add the tomatoes, with their juices, and the sugar. Bring to a simmer over high heat. Reduce the heat to medium-low and cook, uncovered, for 30 minutes, stirring occasionally and breaking up the tomatoes with a wooden spoon. Season with salt and pepper to taste.

# ALL-PURPOSE TOMATO SAUCE

MAKES ABOUT 2-½ CUPS (625 ML)

2 tbsp (30 mL) extra virgin olive oil
3 cloves garlic, thinly sliced
1 can (28 oz/796 mL) whole, peeled tomatoes (preferably San Marzano)
1 tsp (5 mL) granulated sugar
Kosher salt and freshly ground black pepper to taste

# VEGETABLE SIDE DISHES

> We all need to eat more veggies, so let's get creative with a bunch of lovely side dishes.

*Left: Rapini*

## » GARLIC-BASIL SMASHED POTATOES

MAKES 4–6 SERVINGS

1 bag (1-½ lb/680 g) mini
    potatoes
1 tbsp (15 mL) extra virgin olive
    oil, plus more for drizzling
1 tsp (5 mL) flaky sea salt, or to
    taste
Minced cloves from 1 head
    garlic
Chopped leaves from 1 bunch
    fresh basil

This is my favourite way to eat spuds. Look for those small bags of pre-washed mini potatoes. I like the ones that have a mixture of yellow, red and blue potatoes. Food writer Susan Sampson ran this flavour combo in 2005, adapted from a recipe by Food Network star and cookbook author Bob Blumer (bobblumer.com).

Bob, a Torontonian living in California who travels the world in search of food, has this to say: "I brown the potatoes to within an inch of their lives, drizzle with olive oil at the end with wild abandon, and hold back somewhat on the garlic (though this is the first time in my life that I have ever found cause to hold back on garlic)."

In my version, I amp up the garlic and basil, slash the oil and make flaky salt key.

**1.** Preheat the oven to 400°F (200°C). In a small roasting pan or medium baking dish, toss the potatoes with 1 tbsp (15 mL) oil, then sprinkle with salt. Roast in the oven until the potatoes are fork tender inside and crispy outside, 45 to 60 minutes, depending on the size of the potatoes.

**2.** Using a fork, gently press each potato just until it pops. Transfer the potatoes to a serving dish, along with any oil and salt in the roasting pan.

**3.** Add the garlic and basil and, if desired, drizzle with a little more oil. Stir gently until well combined.

## » BROCCOLI AND RUSSET POTATO HASH

MAKES 4–6 SERVINGS

1 russet (baking) potato,
    scrubbed and cut into
    ½-inch (1 cm) dice
1 bunch broccoli (3 stalks),
    stalks peeled and diced, tops
    cut into small florets
¼ cup (60 mL) extra virgin olive
    oil
1 medium yellow onion, diced
1 large clove garlic, minced
1 sprig thyme
Kosher salt and freshly ground
    black pepper to taste
Freshly squeezed lemon juice
    to taste

Canoe, on the 54th floor of the TD Bank Tower, draws Toronto's business elite. Lunching with a reader who won our Eaters' Choice Awards contest in 2003, I ordered grilled Alberta strip loin. It came with green peppercorn sauce, king oyster mushrooms and this hash—described by the chef as a "deconstructed broccoli-stuffed baked potato"—which stole the show. Canoe is part of the Oliver & Bonacini Restaurants empire (oliverbonacini.com).

**1.** In a medium saucepan, combine the potato pieces and enough cold water to cover them. Bring to a boil over high heat. Reduce the heat to medium-low and simmer, covered, until the potato is almost tender, about 10 minutes. Drain the potato well, then spread out on a clean towel to dry and cool slightly.

**2.** Meanwhile, bring a large saucepan of water to a boil over high heat. Add the broccoli and cook until very soft, 5 to 7 minutes. Drain the broccoli well, then spread out on a second clean towel to dry and cool slightly.

**3.** In a large non-stick skillet, heat the oil over medium heat. Add the onion and garlic, and cook, stirring often, until softened, about 7 minutes. Add the broccoli and thyme, and cook, crushing the broccoli with a wooden spoon until the florets and stems are partially crumbled.

**4.** Add the potato and cook, stirring gently, until well mixed and heated through. Discard the thyme sprig, and season with salt, pepper and lemon juice to taste.

This creamy, dreamy mash, from chef Andy Bennett who used to cook in a Canadian-owned gastro-pub in New York City, is the perfect accompaniment to the Guinness-Braised Beef on page 114.

1. In a large pot of lightly salted boiling water, simmer the potatoes until they're tender, about 30 minutes. Drain well, reserving 1 cup (250 mL) cooking liquid. Transfer the potatoes to a large bowl and mash until smooth.

2. In a medium saucepan over medium heat, simmer the parsnips in the cream until they're tender, about 15 minutes, reducing the heat if necessary to prevent the cream from boiling over.

3. Transfer the parsnips and cream to a food processor and purée until smooth.

4. Add the parsnip purée to the potatoes and stir well. If the mash isn't creamy enough, stir in some of the reserved potato cooking liquid.

# PARSNIP AND YUKON GOLD MASH

MAKES 6 SERVINGS

3 lb (1.3 kg) Yukon Gold potatoes, peeled and cut into chunks

1 lb (450 g) parsnips, peeled and cut into thin rounds

1-½ cups (375 mL) whipping or half-and-half cream

"I make this at least once a week using a variety of different vegetables (but still maintaining the basic seasoning)—Brussels sprouts, squash, cabbage, white potatoes, green peas—all in various combinations. I substitute coconut oil for the ghee, and usually add cashews for protein. With a side of brown basmati rice, it's a perfect meal."

**JANE MOORE,** TORONTO

When Geetha Upadhyaya served this spectacular side during a weeknight dinner at her home, I couldn't wait to make it. I adore sweet potatoes, but the addition of fresh curry leaves, dried coconut and black mustard seeds takes them in a whole new flavour direction. Usli is the term used in Karnataka (the Indian state where the family is from) for a simple dry dish with seasonings.

**1.** Steam the sweet potatoes over medium-high heat in a steamer insert in a large saucepan, over 1 inch (2.5 cm) of simmering water, until just starting to soften, 7 to 9 minutes. Alternatively, put them in a microwave-safe bowl, sprinkle with water and cover with a lid or plate. Microwave on high until just starting to soften, 7 to 10 minutes.

**2.** Break the dried chili into 3 pieces over a large non-stick skillet over medium heat, letting the seeds fall into the skillet and dropping in the chili pieces. Add the ghee and mustard seeds to the skillet. When the seeds start to pop, add the curry leaves, and cook, stirring, for 30 seconds.

**3.** Add the sweet potatoes to the skillet. Sprinkle with the coconut, salt, turmeric and chili powder, and cook, stirring, for 2 minutes. Reduce the heat to low and cook, covered, until the sweet potatoes are tender, about 2 minutes.

# GEETHA'S SWEET POTATO USLI «

MAKES 6 SERVINGS

2 lb (900 g) sweet potatoes, scrubbed and cut into ½-inch (1 cm) dice

1 finger-length dried red chili (preferably Kashmiri)

2 tbsp (30 mL) ghee (clarified butter)

1 tsp (5 mL) black mustard seeds

15 fresh curry leaves

3 tbsp (45 mL) unsweetened, desiccated coconut

1 tsp (5 mL) fine sea salt

¼ tsp (1 mL) turmeric

¼ tsp (1 mL) pure Indian chili powder or cayenne

## » BAKED SWEET POTATO WEDGES WITH CHILI MAYO

MAKES 2–3 SERVINGS

2 small sweet potatoes, scrubbed
1 tbsp (15 mL) extra virgin olive oil
¼ cup (60 mL) mayonnaise
1 tbsp (15 mL) Asian chili-garlic sauce or sambal oelek (chili sauce), or more to taste

This is my favourite way to eat Ontario-grown sweet potatoes, which are often mislabelled "yams." The recipe doubles easily and also makes a great appetizer or snack.

To find out more about Ontario vegetables, check out Foodland Ontario's produce fact sheets and recipes at foodland.gov.on.ca.

**1.** Preheat the oven to 400°F (200°C). Line a baking sheet with parchment paper.

**2.** Cut the sweet potatoes in half lengthwise, then cut each half lengthwise into 4 fingers. In a medium bowl, toss the sweet potato wedges with the oil.

**3.** Arrange the wedges in a single layer on the prepared baking sheet, then bake in the oven for 20 minutes. Flip the potatoes and bake until tender and beginning to brown, about 20 minutes.

**4.** Meanwhile, in a small bowl, whisk together the mayo and chili-garlic or chili sauce until smooth. Serve the sweet potato wedges with chili mayo for dipping.

Eat local by buying Ontario portobellos, tomatoes and cheese for this recipe which is adapted from one by Mushrooms Canada (mushrooms.ca). It stars earthy, meaty portobellos which, like all mushrooms, should be refrigerated in brown paper (not plastic) bags so they can breathe.

**1.** In a medium bowl, gently stir together the tomato, avocado and feta.

**2.** In a small bowl, whisk together 2 tbsp (30 mL) oil, the vinegar and pepper to taste. Add to the tomato mixture and toss gently to coat. Set aside.

**3.** Preheat the broiler to high. Brush the mushroom caps on both sides with the remaining 2 tbsp (30 mL) oil. Arrange, gill sides down, on a oiled, rimmed baking sheet and broil until the mushrooms caps are tender, about 4 minutes per side.

**4.** Divide the mushroom caps, gill sides up, among 4 or 8 plates. Top each with the tomato salsa, dividing evenly.

# PORTOBELLO CAPS WITH SALSA ≪

MAKES 4-8 SERVINGS

1 large tomato, quartered, seeded and diced

1 avocado, peeled, pitted and diced

¾ cup (175 mL) crumbled feta cheese or chèvre (soft unripened goat cheese; about 3 oz/85 g)

¼ cup (60 mL) extra virgin olive oil

1 tbsp (15 mL) white wine vinegar

Freshly ground black pepper to taste

4 large or 8 medium portobello mushrooms, stems removed

## » THE SAUCY LADY'S MUSHROOMS AND ONIONS

MAKES 6 SERVINGS

1 lb (450 g) mushrooms
  (creminis, king oyster and/or
  shiitake mushrooms)
⅓ cup (80 mL) soy sauce
2 tbsp (30 mL) peeled, minced
  ginger
2 tbsp (30 mL) Asian hot sauce,
  such as chili-garlic sauce,
  sambal oelek (chili sauce) or
  Sriracha, or to taste
2 tbsp (30 mL) vegetable oil
4 large cloves garlic, minced
1 tbsp (15 mL) sesame seeds,
  toasted
1 tbsp (15 mL) sesame oil
3 medium yellow onions, halved
  and thinly sliced

For eight years, I grudgingly choked down mushrooms in the line of duty until one day, after visiting a mushroom farm for a Saucy Lady column, I suddenly—inexplicably—liked them. Now I crave them, usually alongside steak but sometimes on their own. I gravitate to creminis, king oyster mushrooms or shiitakes, and all work well in this dish, individually or as a mixture.

Toast sesame seeds in a small, dry skillet over medium heat until lightly browned. You can turn this fiery side into a vegetarian main dish for four by serving it on brown rice.

**1.** Cut the cremini mushrooms into halves or quarters (depending on size), slice the king oyster mushrooms, and remove the stems from the shiitakes and tear their caps into pieces.

**2.** In a large bowl, whisk together the soy sauce, ginger, hot sauce, vegetable oil, garlic, sesame seeds and sesame oil. Add the mushrooms and onions, and toss to coat well. Let stand at room temperature, tossing occasionally, for up to 1 hour.

**3.** Heat a large non-stick skillet over medium-high heat. Add the mushrooms and onions with their marinade, and cook, stirring often, until the mushrooms are tender and the onions are browned, 10 to 15 minutes.

*Right: King oyster mushrooms*

Once you've tried Nick auf der Mauer's way with rapini (a.k.a. broccoli rabe), it will become your go-to green. Nick blanches the bitterness out of the rapini, then pan-fries it with onions, garlic and dried chilies. It's great as a vegetable side but, at his gourmet sandwich shop Porchetta & Co. (porchettaco.com), Nick tucks it in a porchetta sandwich with crackling, truffle sauce and grainy mustard.

# PORCHETTA & CO.'S RAPINI WITH GARLIC AND CHILI

**MAKES 4 SERVINGS**

1 bunch rapini (about 1-½ lb/680 g)
2 tbsp (30 mL) extra virgin olive oil
1 medium yellow onion, finely chopped
3 large cloves garlic, thinly sliced
½ tsp (2 mL) dried red chili flakes
Kosher salt and freshly ground black pepper to taste

**1.** Trim and discard the bottom 1 inch (2.5 cm) of the rapini stems. Chop the remaining stems and leaves into 2-inch (5 cm) pieces and rinse well.

**2.** Bring a large pot of water to a boil and add the rapini. Return the water to a boil and cook for 1 minute. Drain well in a colander and spread the rapini out on a clean towel to dry and cool slightly.

**3.** In a large skillet, heat the oil over medium heat. Add the onion and cook, stirring often, until golden, about 7 minutes. Add the garlic and chilies, and cook, stirring often, until browned, about 3 minutes.

**4.** Add the rapini to the skillet and cook, stirring often, until the rapini is tender and heated through, 2 to 3 minutes. (If the pan is dry, add a splash of water.) Taste and season with salt and pepper if necessary.

## » CHEESY CAULIFLOWER (OR BROCCOLI)

MAKES 6 SERVINGS

1 large head cauliflower, broken
  into large florets, or 3
  large stalks broccoli, stalks
  trimmed and thinly sliced
  and heads broken into large
  florets
1 tbsp (15 mL) unsalted butter
1 tbsp (15 mL) all-purpose flour
1 cup (250 mL) milk
½ cup (125 mL) coarsely grated
  Beemster cheese

Thanks to my mom, I grew up pouring a warm blanket of orange cheddar sauce over my cauliflower and broccoli. Now, presiding over a family of cheeseheads, I splurge on Beemster, an aged Dutch Gouda-style cheese that's widely available in supermarkets, for my sauce.

**1.** Steam the cauliflower or broccoli over medium-high heat in a steamer insert in a large saucepan, over 1 inch (2.5 cm) of simmering water, until tender, 8 to 10 minutes for the cauliflower, 4 to 6 minutes for the broccoli. Transfer the vegetable to a serving dish.

**2.** Meanwhile, melt the butter in a small saucepan over medium heat. Add the flour and cook, whisking constantly, until lightly browned, 45 to 60 seconds. Slowly pour in the milk, whisking constantly.

**3.** Add the cheese, and cook, whisking often and reducing the heat to medium-low if necessary, until the sauce has thickened and is smooth, 8 to 10 minutes.

**4.** Either drizzle the cheese sauce over the vegetable in the dish or pour the sauce into a gravy boat or bowl and serve alongside the vegetable.

I troll the Internet, food magazines and cookbooks for recipes and flavour ideas that dazzle with their simplicity. This magical side dish, adapted from one served at Sam Mogannam's Bi-Rite Market in San Francisco via *Food & Wine* magazine, is a revelation.

Tahini, a ground paste of sesame seeds, is the key ingredient in hummus and not used nearly enough elsewhere. Some brands are thick and gloopy, but I prefer my tahini thin and pourable.

# WARM TAHINI CARROTS

MAKES 4–6 SERVINGS

1-½ lb (680 g) carrots, peeled and thickly sliced
¼ cup (60 mL) well-stirred tahini (sesame paste)
¼ cup (60 mL) extra virgin olive oil
¼ cup (60 mL) fresh lemon juice
2 tbsp (30 mL) water, or more as needed
3 large cloves garlic, minced

1. Steam the carrots over medium-high heat in a steamer insert in a large saucepan, over 1 inch (2.5 cm) of simmering water, until just tender, about 6 minutes. Transfer the carrots to a serving bowl.

2. In a medium bowl, whisk together the tahini, oil, lemon juice and 2 tbsp (30 mL) water until smooth, adding more water if necessary to make a pourable consistency. Whisk in the garlic.

3. Drizzle the tahini mixture over the carrots, tossing to coat well. Serve the carrots warm or at room temperature. You may not need all the tahini mixture so refrigerate any remaining dressing in an airtight container for another use, such as a dip for raw veggies.

## » CUMIN CARROTS WITH CILANTRO VINAIGRETTE

MAKES 4 SERVINGS

**Cilantro Vinaigrette**

1 tbsp (15 mL) extra virgin olive
   oil
Juice of ½ lemon
1 tbsp (15 mL) liquid honey
3 tbsp (45 mL) chopped cilantro

**Carrots**

1 tbsp (15 mL) extra virgin olive
   oil
1 large clove garlic, minced
¼ tsp (1 mL) ground cumin
1 lb (450 g) carrots, peeled,
   thinly sliced in rounds
Sea salt and freshly ground
   black pepper to taste

I was at a gathering of local food enthusiasts at the Gambrel Barn in Country Heritage Park in Milton in 2004, when Toronto chef Gary Hoyer served this flavour-packed creation using Ontario carrots. The key is to keep the carrots crunchy. Gary is now a principal with GNH Hospitality Consultants and a professor at George Brown College.

**1.** For the Cilantro Vinaigrette, whisk together the oil, lemon juice and honey in a small bowl, then whisk in the cilantro.

**2.** For the carrots, heat the oil in a large non-stick skillet over medium-high heat. Add the garlic and cumin, and cook, stirring, for 2 minutes. Add the carrots and cook, stirring, until they're only half cooked, about 4 minutes, depending on the thickness of the slices.

**3.** Transfer the carrots to a serving bowl. Add the vinaigrette and toss well. Taste and season with salt and pepper if necessary. Serve the carrots warm or at room temperature.

In this recipe chef Matthew Kantor (mattkantor.ca) combines four ordinary flavours into something unique. As he says, "It just works." Matt caters with his Little Kitchen and Ghost Chef businesses, and creates pop-up dining experiences with his Secret Pickle Supper Club. If you like, use chanterelles, shiitakes or king oyster mushrooms instead of creminis.

1. Bring a large saucepan of water to a boil over high heat. Add the asparagus and cook until tender-crisp, about 2 minutes for thin stalks, 3 minutes for fat. Drain the asparagus well.

2. Meanwhile, in a large skillet, heat the oil over medium-high heat. Add the mushrooms and cook, stirring occasionally, until tender, 6 to 8 minutes. Add the blueberries and asparagus, and cook, stirring gently, until heated through, about 3 minutes.

3. Transfer the asparagus mixture to a serving platter. Using a stainless steel rasp or other zester, finely grate as much zest from the lemon as you like over the vegetables. Season with flaky sea salt (if using).

# ASPARAGUS WITH MUSHROOMS AND BLUEBERRIES

MAKES 4 SERVINGS

1 lb (450 g) asparagus, tough ends trimmed
3 tbsp (45 mL) extra virgin olive oil
12 cremini mushrooms, trimmed and quartered
24 fresh blueberries
1 lemon, washed
Flaky sea salt to taste (optional)

This brilliant use of cucumbers comes from Francisco Alejandri, Toronto's most dazzling Mexican chef. He served it at Agave y Aguacate, a takeout stand he used to run in a Latin-themed food court in Kensington Market. Francisco calls it White Chalupas, with chalupa being the Spanish word for a canoe-like boat.

Manchego is a firm Spanish sheep's milk cheese, but you could substitute Pecorino Romano. Pequín chilies are small, red, hot, smoky dried chilies. Buy them whole in Latin grocery stores and grind them in a coffee grinder reserved for spices.

**1.** Peel the cucumbers and cut them in half lengthwise. Scoop out and discard the seeds, and pat the cucumbers dry. Put them, cut sides up, on a serving platter and season with salt to taste.

**2.** In a small bowl, combine the onion, lime juice and vinegar. Divide the onion mixture among the cavities of the cucumbers. Sprinkle the cheese evenly over the cucumbers, then sprinkle ground chili to taste down the centre of each one.

# FRANCISCO'S MEXICAN CUCUMBERS «

MAKES 4 SERVINGS

2 field cucumbers
Kosher salt to taste
6 tbsp (90 mL) finely diced white onion
2 tbsp (30 mL) fresh lime juice
2 tbsp (30 mL) cider vinegar
¾ cup (185 mL) finely grated Manchego cheese (about 2 oz/60 g)
Pure chili powder (such as pequín or chipotle) or cayenne or dried red chili flakes, to taste

# DESSERTS, COOKIES AND CAKES

Sugar, chocolate, fruit, butter. . . No explanation needed.

*Left: Augie's watermelon-lemonade ice pops*

## STICKY DATE PUDDING WITH WARM TOFFEE SAUCE

**READERS' CHOICE**

MAKES 8–10 SERVINGS

### Cake

2 cups (500 mL) water
10 oz (285 g) pitted Medjool
    dates, chopped
1-½ tsp (7 mL) baking soda
2 cups (500 mL) all-purpose
    flour
2 tsp (10 mL) fine sea salt
½ tsp (2 mL) baking powder
½ tsp (2 mL) ground ginger
1 cup (250 mL) granulated sugar
6 tbsp (90 mL) unsalted butter,
    at room temperature
3 large eggs

### Toffee Sauce

¾ cup (185 mL) unsalted butter
1-¼ cups (310 mL) packed light
    brown sugar
1 cup (250 mL) whipping cream
½ tsp (2 mL) vanilla

"This dessert is extremely delicious. I have made it countless times for various occasions and everyone especially enjoys the accompanying toffee sauce which has resulted in many requests for the recipe."

**NASREEN RAZVI,** MARKHAM, ONT.

Food writer Susan Sampson found this in 2004 on Prince Edward Island at the Dalvay By The Sea hotel (dalvaybythesea.com). "We think the dessert conjures up memories in all who eat it of comfortable times in their lives. It remains popular to this day," reports Dalvay's general manager Audrey Firth.

**1.** For the cake, preheat the oven to 375°F (190°C). Butter and flour an 8-inch (2 L) square baking dish.

**2.** In a medium saucepan, bring the water and dates to a boil over high heat. Reduce the heat to medium-low and simmer, uncovered, for 5 minutes. Remove the saucepan from the heat. Stir in the baking soda and let stand for 20 minutes.

**3.** In a medium bowl, sift together the flour, salt, baking powder and ginger.

**4.** In a large bowl, and using an electric mixer on high speed, beat together the sugar and butter until fluffy. Beat in the eggs, 1 at a time, beating well after each addition.

**5.** With the mixer on low speed, gradually beat in the flour mixture in 3 additions, beating after each addition just until combined. Add the date mixture and stir with a wooden spoon just until combined.

**6.** Pour the batter into the prepared dish. Set the dish in a shallow roasting pan and add enough hot water to reach halfway up the sides of the dish. Bake in the centre of the oven until a cake tester comes out clean, 50 to 60 minutes. Remove the dish from the roasting pan and put on a wire rack.

**7.** Meanwhile, for the Toffee Sauce, melt the butter in a medium saucepan over medium heat. Add the sugar and bring to a boil, stirring occasionally. Stir in the cream and return to the boil. Reduce the heat to medium-low and simmer, stirring occasionally, until slightly thickened, about 5 minutes. Remove the saucepan from the heat and stir in the vanilla.

**8.** Cut the warm pudding into squares and serve drizzled with sauce.

"My all-time favourite dessert to make at Christmas, because eggnog is only available during that time, is your breadnog pudding. I use panettone as the bread base and my goodness, this recipe is a hit!"

**ANGELA ADAMS,** MARKHAM, ONT.

In 2010, I invited three student chefs from Niagara College's Canadian Food and Wine Institute to the *Star* test kitchen for an eggnog challenge. Working with Organic Meadow eggnog (which truly is the tastiest), the students had 90 minutes to create something special. Shannon Brubacher, now a Niagara culinary graduate, won with this festive bread pudding.

**1.** For the Breadnog Pudding, preheat the oven to 400°F (200°C). Butter an 11- x 7-inch (2 L) baking dish. Sprinkle the sugar all over the surface of the dish.

**2.** In a small saucepan, bring the raisins and rum to a simmer over medium heat. Simmer until the raisins are plump and the rum has nearly all evaporated, about 10 minutes. Remove the saucepan from the heat and set aside.

**3.** With the tip of a paring knife, scrape out the tiny seeds from the vanilla bean, discarding the bean. In a large bowl, whisk together the eggnog, eggs and vanilla seeds or vanilla. Add the raisin mixture and the bread, and stir well. Let stand for 10 minutes to moisten the bread, then stir again. Tip the mixture into the prepared dish, spreading it out to fill the dish. Bake in the oven until puffed, golden and firm, about 45 minutes.

**4.** Meanwhile for the Eggnog-Pecan Sauce, scrape out the tiny seeds from the vanilla bean with the tip of a paring knife, discarding the bean. In a medium saucepan, melt the butter over medium heat. Add the flour and cook, stirring constantly, until light brown, about 6 minutes.

**5.** Add the sugar, milk, cream, rum and vanilla seeds or vanilla. Bring to a boil, whisking constantly, until the sauce thickens and is a caramel colour. Remove the saucepan from the heat and let the sauce cool for 5 minutes. Stir in the pecans and eggnog.

**6.** Spoon portions of warm Breadnog Pudding onto individual plates and serve with the sauce drizzled over the top.

# BREADNOG PUDDING WITH EGGNOG-PECAN SAUCE

**READERS' CHOICE**

MAKES 8–10 SERVINGS

### Breadnog Pudding
1 tbsp (15 mL) granulated sugar
1 cup (250 mL) Thompson or sultana raisins
½ cup (125 mL) dark rum
½ vanilla bean, split lengthwise, or 2 tsp (10 mL) pure vanilla extract
5 cups (1.25 L) eggnog
4 large eggs
1 loaf challah (egg) bread, cut into 1-inch (2.5 cm) cubes (about 10 cups/2.5 L)

### Eggnog-Pecan Sauce
½ vanilla bean, split lengthwise, or 2 tsp (10 mL) pure vanilla extract
2 tbsp (30 mL) unsalted butter
2 tsp (10 mL) all-purpose flour
1-½ cups (375 mL) packed light brown sugar
¾ cup (185 mL) homogenized (3.25%) milk
¾ cup (185 mL) whipping cream
1 tbsp (15 mL) dark rum
½ cup (125 mL) pecan halves, lightly toasted
½ cup (125 mL) eggnog

## » THE BROTHERS' RICE PUDDING

MAKES 6 SERVINGS

4 cups (1 L) 2% or homogenized (3.25%) milk, plus more if needed
1 cup (250 mL) long-grain parboiled rice, rinsed and drained
½ cup (125 mL) granulated sugar
1 large egg, at room temperature
1 tsp (5 mL) pure vanilla extract
3 tbsp (45 mL) raisins (optional)
Ground cinnamon for sprinkling

Restaurant critic Amy Pataki adored unpretentious, old-school diner The Brothers, on Yonge Street, just south of Bloor. The owners, who were cousins rather than brothers, shared this recipe with her just before the diner closed in 2000. On the menu at The Brothers, this creamy treat was sometimes called by its Greek name rizogalo.

**1.** In a medium, heavy-bottomed saucepan, bring 4 cups (1 L) milk to a simmer over medium heat. Add the rice and sugar, and simmer gently, uncovered, until the rice is almost cooked through but still a little chewy, about 30 minutes, stirring with a wooden spoon occasionally at the beginning and more frequently toward the end of cooking time. You may need to reduce the heat to medium-low toward the end to prevent the mixture from sticking.

**2.** In a small bowl, whisk together the egg and vanilla. Whisk 2 tbsp (30 mL) of the hot milk from the saucepan into the egg mixture, continuing to whisk until smooth. Stir the egg mixture back into the rice mixture. (Tempering the beaten egg with the hot milk first prevents it from scrambling when you add it to the rice mixture.)

**3.** Reduce the heat to medium-low and cook, stirring constantly, until the pudding has thickened, about 2 minutes. Stir in the raisins (if using).

**4.** Transfer the pudding to a medium bowl and let cool, uncovered, stirring occasionally, for 30 minutes. Serve the pudding warm, generously sprinkled with cinnamon and thinned with more milk if desired. If you prefer, refrigerate the pudding until chilled and serve it cold.

I make no excuses for having two rice puddings in this book as it's one of my favourite comfort foods. For this one, from Victoria's restaurant in Le Méridien King Edward hotel, executive chef Daniel Schick uses a vanilla bean instead of vanilla extract, and arborio rice instead of long-grain parboiled rice. Arborio is a starchy Italian short-grain rice that also features in risotto.

1. With the tip of a paring knife, scrape out the tiny seeds from the vanilla bean. Put the seeds and bean in a large, heavy-bottomed saucepan with the milk, rice and sugar. Bring to a boil over medium-high heat.

2. Reduce the heat to low or medium-low and simmer gently, uncovered, until the rice is soft and resembles a loose risotto, 30 to 40 minutes, stirring with a wooden spoon occasionally at the beginning and more frequently toward the end of cooking time.

3. Transfer the pudding to a medium bowl. Remove and discard the vanilla bean. Press a piece of plastic wrap directly on the surface of the pudding to prevent a skin from forming. Let cool to room temperature, about 1 hour.

4. Using a rubber spatula, gently stir in the cream. Serve warm or, if you prefer, refrigerate the pudding until chilled and serve it cold.

# THE KING EDDY'S RICE PUDDING

«

MAKES 4 SERVINGS

½ vanilla bean, split lengthwise
3 cups (750 mL) homogenized (3.25%) milk
½ cup (125 mL) arborio rice
½ cup (125 mL) granulated sugar
¾ cup (185 mL) whipping cream

"I have never liked pumpkin pie, but I make it for everyone else. When I tried the Ultimate Pumpkin Pie, however, I began to understand the appeal. It has a wonderfully rich flavour that doesn't mask the pumpkin."

**CHRISTINA KRAMER,** TORONTO

My former *Star* food compatriot, Susan Sampson (thefarelady.com), who now writes cookbooks, created this swoon-worthy pumpkin pie as a reaction to boring supermarket pie.

**1.** For the pumpkin pie, roll out the dough and line a buttered 10-inch (25 cm) deep-dish pie plate. Crimp the edges, then refrigerate until firm, at least 30 minutes. Preheat the oven to 400°F (200°C).

**2.** Cover the pie shell with foil or parchment paper, then top with pie weights, dried beans or uncooked rice. Bake in the bottom third of the oven for 5 minutes. Remove the weights and foil or parchment and return the pie shell to the oven. Continue to bake until the surface starts to look dry but the pastry is not browned, about 5 minutes. Remove the pie plate from the oven and put it on a wire rack. Reduce the oven temperature to 325°F (160°C).

**3.** In a large bowl, whisk together the pumpkin, brown and granulated sugars, flour, cinnamon, salt, ginger, nutmeg, allspice and pepper. Add the cream, orange juice, bourbon, rum or whisky (if using) and vanilla, and whisk to blend. Whisk in the eggs until smooth. Pour the pumpkin mixture into the pie shell. Bake in the centre of the oven for 1 hour.

**4.** In a small bowl, stir together the walnuts and toffee bits. Sprinkle the mixture evenly over the pie. Continue to bake until the filling firms up and puffs slightly at the sides but is still a bit wobbly in the centre, 15 to 30 minutes. Let the pie cool to room temperature on a wire rack.

**5.** For the Gingered Whipped Cream, whip the cream in a large bowl with an electric mixer until soft peaks form. Add the icing sugar, then whip until firm peaks form. If you like, garnish the whole pie with a dollop of cream and a sprinkling of ginger. Serve slices topped with the remaining cream and ginger.

# ULTIMATE PUMPKIN PIE

**READERS' CHOICE**

MAKES 6–8 SERVINGS

### Pumpkin Pie
1 ball pastry dough (page 211) or enough for a 10-inch (25 cm) single-crust deep-dish pie
1-¾ cups (435 mL) canned pure pumpkin
⅔ cup (160 mL) packed dark brown sugar
¼ cup (60 mL) granulated sugar
1 tbsp (15 mL) all-purpose flour
1 tsp (15 mL) ground cinnamon
½ tsp (2 mL) table salt
½ tsp (2 mL) ground ginger
½ tsp (2 mL) ground nutmeg
¼ tsp (1 mL) ground allspice
Pinch black pepper
1 cup (250 mL) whipping cream
⅓ cup (80 mL) orange juice
2 tbsp (30 mL) bourbon, dark rum or whisky (optional)
1 tsp (5 mL) pure vanilla extract
3 large eggs, beaten
½ cup (125 mL) walnut pieces, lightly toasted and chopped
¼ cup (60 mL) toffee bits

### Gingered Whipped Cream
1 cup (250 mL) whipping cream
1 tbsp (15 mL) icing sugar
¼ cup (60 mL) finely diced crystallized ginger

## ›› MACKENZIE FAMILY GRATED APPLE PIE

MAKES 8 SERVINGS

2 balls pastry dough (page 211)
   or enough for a 10-inch
   (25 cm) double-crust deep-
   dish pie
10 McIntosh or Granny Smith
   apples (about 3-½ lb/1.6 kg),
   peeled, cored and grated on
   large holes of a box grater
   (about 6 cups/1.5 L loosely
   packed)
⅔ cup (160 mL) granulated
   sugar
2 tbsp (30 mL) all-purpose flour
1 tbsp (15 mL) ground cinnamon
Pinch kosher salt
1 to 2 tsp (5 to 10 mL) cold
   unsalted butter, cut into
   small pieces

This is my husband, Rick MacKenzie's, signature dish. His crust is light, flaky and made with lard, his apples are grated instead of sliced, and his pie plate is deep-dish. He learned to make pie this way from his mom, Margaret MacKenzie, and loves to make all kinds of pies, but this is the one I always request.

**1.** Butter or grease a 10-inch (25 cm) deep-dish pie plate. On a lightly floured surface, keeping the remaining pastry refrigerated, roll out half of the pastry to an 11- to 12-inch (28 to 30 cm) circle; jagged edges are okay. (If the pastry seems too sticky to roll, refrigerate it for 1 to 2 hours, then try again.) Use a large rubber spatula to loosen the pastry from the counter. Carefully transfer it to the prepared pie plate and pat it into place.

**2.** Cut or pull off most of the excess overhang, leaving a little in place. Use the excess pastry to patch any holes in the crust, dipping your fingers in cold water to seal any patches. Refrigerate the pie plate so the pastry remains cold while you make the filling. Preheat the oven to 450°F (230°C).

**3.** In a large bowl, combine the apples, sugar, flour, cinnamon and salt, and stir with a wooden spoon until well mixed. Tip the apple mixture into the prepared pie plate and dot the filling with the butter.

**4.** On a lightly floured surface, roll out the remaining pastry as above and place over the pie. Use a knife to cut off most of the excess overhang then, with your finger and thumb, crimp and seal the edges. Using a fork, make 6 steam vents in the pie.

**5.** Bake the pie in the centre of the oven for 20 minutes. Reduce the temperature to 375°F (190°C) and continue to bake until the top is golden and the filling is bubbly, 30 to 45 minutes. Remove the pie from the oven and let cool on a wire rack to your desired temperature. The pie can be served warm, at room temperature or cold.

My husband Rick and his mom swear by a modified version of the pie crust recipe on the Tenderflake lard package but, for reasons lost in family lore, they don't use an egg. The key is to keep the lard and pastry as cold as possible. The MacKenzies even chill their pie plates. "I go for cold, cold, cold," reports Rick. "Winter pie baking is best."

**1.** In a large bowl, stir together the flour and salt. Using a pastry cutter or 2 knives, mix in the lard in 4 to 6 additions until pea-sized clumps form (some larger clumps are okay; the Tenderflake instructions and Margaret prefer oatmeal-sized clumps).

**2.** Put the vinegar in a 1-cup (250 mL) measuring cup and add enough cold water to make 1 cup (250 mL). Gradually stir the vinegar mixture into the flour mixture, stirring with a wooden spoon and adding only enough liquid to make the dough cling together.

**3.** Gather the dough into a ball and divide into 5 even-size pieces. Form each piece into a ball and wrap each ball in plastic wrap or put them in individual plastic bags, then refrigerate for up to 1 day or freeze for up to 6 months.

**4.** When you're ready to use the dough, thaw it out overnight in the fridge, then roll it out as instructed in the MacKenzie Family Grated Apple Pie recipe (page 211). If it doesn't roll easily, bring it to room temperature.

# MACKENZIE FAMILY PIE CRUST  «

MAKES 5 BALLS OF DOUGH
(ENOUGH FOR 2 DOUBLE AND
1 SINGLE 10-INCH (25 CM)
DEEP-DISH PIES)

6 cups (1.5 L) all-purpose flour
2 tsp (10 mL) table salt
1 lb (450 g) cold lard (preferably Tenderflake), cut into large pieces
1 tbsp (15 mL) white vinegar
Cold water as needed

# » ROYAL MCINTOSH CRUMBLE

MAKES 8–10 SERVINGS

## Filling

2 McIntosh apples, peeled, cored and cut into 1-inch (2.5 cm) cubes

2 Crispin apples, peeled, cored and cut into 1-inch (2.5 cm) cubes

2 Honeycrisp apples, peeled, cored and cut into 1-inch (2.5 cm) cubes

6 tbsp (90 mL) granulated sugar

1 tbsp (15 mL) ground cinnamon

¼ tsp (1 mL) pure vanilla extract

2 tbsp (30 mL) cold unsalted butter, cut into small pieces

## Topping

½ cup (125 mL) packed light brown sugar

¼ cup (60 mL) cold unsalted butter, cut into small pieces

½ cup (125 mL) all-purpose flour

½ cup (125 mL) large flake oats

¼ cup (60 mL) chopped blanched (skinless) almonds

Steffan Howard, executive chef of the Pegasus Hospitality Group (pegasushospitality.ca), created this crumble for the Royal Agricultural Winter Fair in 2011 to celebrate the 100th anniversary of the McIntosh apple, which was discovered by farmer John McIntosh in Dundela, Ontario. As well as McIntosh, Steffan includes two other Ontario apples—Crispin and Honeycrisp. Each variety cooks to a different level of softness to create an interesting texture, and chopped almonds in the topping create unexpected crunch.

**1.** For the filling, preheat the oven to 350°F (180°C). Butter a 9- x 13-inch (23 - x 33-cm) baking dish.

**2.** Toss together all the apples in a large bowl until well combined. In a small bowl, stir together the sugar, cinnamon and vanilla. Add the sugar mixture to the apples and toss to coat well. Spread the apple mixture out in the prepared dish and dot evenly with the butter.

**3.** For the topping, using your fingertips, rub together the sugar and butter in a medium bowl until the mixture resembles coarse crumbs. Add the flour, oats and almonds, and mix well. Spoon or sprinkle the topping evenly over the filling.

**4.** Cover the dish loosely with foil and bake in the centre of the oven for 15 minutes. Remove the foil and continue baking until the topping is golden, the apples are tender and their juices start to seep out around the topping, 35 to 45 minutes. Remove from the oven and let cool slightly. Serve warm or at room temperature.

I found Janet Dimond and Augie's Gourmet Ice Pops (augiesicepops.com) at the Evergreen Brick Works Farmers' Market in 2011 and fell in love with her creative flavours. She shared this recipe, but you can experiment with all kinds of fresh fruits and herbs, cane sugar and honey. If you don't have ice pop molds, make the ice pops in Dixie cups using wooden Popsicle sticks.

**1.** In a small saucepan over low heat, heat the sugar and water, stirring often, until the sugar has dissolved, about 5 minutes. Refrigerate this sugar syrup until cold. Spoon out ½ cup (125 mL) plus 1 tbsp (15 mL) and reserve for the ice pops, using the remainder (about ¼ cup/60 mL) in another recipe or discarding it.

**2.** In a large bowl or measuring cup, combine the reserved sugar syrup, puréed watermelon, lemon zest, lemon juice, mint and salt.

**3.** Pour the mixture into the ice pop molds, leaving a ¼-inch (6 mm) headspace in each for expansion. Cover with the lids (that have sticks attached) and freeze the ice pops until firm, 5 to 8 hours.

**4.** If your ice pop molds don't come with sticks, freeze the filled molds for 2 hours or until wooden Popsicle sticks inserted into the semi-frozen ice pops stand on their own. Freeze until firm, 3 to 6 hours more.

**5.** When the ice pops are firm, dip the bottoms of the ice pop molds into a bowl of hot water for up to 30 seconds to loosen the ice pops. Remove the ice pops from the molds. Eat immediately, or wrap individually in plastic wrap then store in a freezer bag in the freezer for up to 3 weeks.

# AUGIE'S WATERMELON-LEMONADE ICE POPS

《

MAKES ABOUT 16

½ cup (125 mL) cane or granulated sugar
½ cup (125 mL) water
4 cups (1 L) puréed, strained watermelon
Finely grated zest of 2 lemons
½ cup (125 mL) fresh lemon juice (from about 3 lemons)
5 mint leaves, finely chopped
Pinch kosher salt
16 ice pop molds (each about 3 oz/85 g) with lids and sticks
Wooden Popsicle sticks (optional)

## » MEXICAN LIME CHARLOTTE

MAKES 12 SERVINGS

2 cans (each 370 mL)
    evaporated milk
2 cans (each 300 mL) sweetened
    condensed milk
1 cup (250 mL) fresh lime juice
    (from about 8 large limes)
About 60 Maria or Rich Tea
    cookies
Finely grated zest of 2 limes
    (preferably dark green parts),
    or more to taste
Freshly squeezed lime juice to
    taste
Fruity extra virgin olive oil to
    taste

People went insane for this knockout, no-bake dessert, the creation of Mexican-Torontonian chef Francisco Alejandri, who used to run takeout stand Agave y Aguacate in Kensington Market. After a few hours, the cookies, bathed in a rich and creamy lime mixture, disintegrate into a cake-like texture.

It's hard to be precise about how many Maria cookies (a.k.a. Rich Tea cookies or biscuits) you'll need. (Mexican Maria cookies—especially Francisco's favourite, Gamesa brand—are slightly sweeter and smaller), but aim for three to four layers and be sure to cover each with the milk mixture.

**1.** Whisk together the evaporated and condensed milks in a large stainless steel bowl. Add 1 cup (250 mL) lime juice (the mixture will look curdled at first), then whisk vigorously until thickened and smooth, about 1 minute.

**2.** Ladle 1-¼ cups (310 mL) of the milk mixture over the bottom of a 9- x 13-inch (23- x 33-cm) dish, tilting the dish and spreading with a rubber spatula, if necessary, so the milk mixture covers the bottom of the dish evenly.

**3.** Gently arrange 1 layer of cookies, side by side and barely touching, over the milk mixture, breaking some of the cookies in half as needed to make them fit. Ladle 1 cup (250 mL) milk mixture over the layer of cookies, spreading it gently with the spatula to make sure the cookies are completely covered. (You may need to add up to ¼ cup/ 60 mL more milk mixture to cover the cookie layer.)

**4.** Continue to layer the cookies and milk mixture, alternating the areas where the whole and broken cookies are. (You should have 3 or 4 cookie layers.) Finish with a layer of milk mixture.

**5.** Cover the dish with plastic wrap, making sure the wrap doesn't touch the dessert. Refrigerate until set, at least 3 hours or up to 2 days.

**6.** Just before serving, use a stainless steel rasp or other zester to zest the limes directly over the dessert (if you do this in advance, the zest will dry out). Drizzle evenly with lime juice and oil. To serve, cut into squares and serve on individual plates.

While backpacking in Thailand in the 1990s, I fell in love with "banana pancakes" made by Muslim street vendors using Indian bread-like wrappers and a drizzle of condensed milk. In Thailand, these are cut into bite-size squares and skewered on toothpicks, but, served whole, they make a unique dessert.

It took me years to find a good recipe but this one, adapted from one that Yaowalak and Jerry Good feature on their website importfood.com, makes the grade. Thai street food is usually fried in margarine so be sure to use it for an authentic flavour.

# THAI BANANA ROTIS

«

MAKES 8

½ cup (125 mL) cold water
1 large egg
1 tbsp (15 mL) granulated sugar
1 tbsp (15 mL) sweetened condensed milk, plus more for drizzling
½ tsp (2 mL) fine sea salt
2 cups (500 mL) all-purpose flour
1 tbsp (15 mL) unsalted butter, melted
Canola oil for greasing
8 tsp (40 mL) margarine, or more as needed
4 bananas, peeled and thinly sliced

**1.** In a small bowl, whisk together the water, egg, sugar, 1 tbsp (15 mL) condensed milk and salt.

**2.** Put the flour in a medium bowl and make a well in the centre. Pour in the water mixture and stir with a wooden spoon until the dough comes together. Drizzle with the butter then, using your hands, form the dough into a ball. Turn the ball out onto an unfloured work surface and knead until it is soft and elastic, 3 to 5 minutes. Lightly grease the ball of dough with oil and return it to the bowl. Let stand, uncovered, for 30 minutes.

**3.** Twist and break the dough into 8 even-size pieces, form each into a ball and coat with oil. (The balls of dough can be stored in an airtight container at room temperature for up to 6 hours.)

**4.** Using a rolling pin, roll 1 ball of dough as thinly as possible into a jagged-edged 10-inch (25 cm) circle (some holes are okay), repeatedly oiling your hands and the dough lightly and pulling the dough with your fingers to help stretch it. Cover the roti with a damp cloth. Repeat with the remaining balls of dough.

**5.** Heat a large non-stick skillet over medium-high heat and add about 1 tsp (5 mL) margarine. Lay 1 roti in the skillet (it will immediately start to shrink) and quickly spread banana slices over the centre, using half a banana per roti. (If your roti is smaller than 5 inches/12.5 cm, adjust the amount of filling accordingly.) Fold the edges of the roti in over the filling to form a 5-inch (12.5 cm) square packet, flattening the packet with a spatula. Cook, turning once, until the roti is browned in spots and crispy, about 2 minutes, reducing the heat if the roti browns too much.

**6.** Transfer the roti to a serving platter, drizzle with condensed milk and keep warm. Repeat with the remaining rotis and bananas.

Since 2008, from December 1 through 24, we've run a wildly popular daily Advent Cookie Calendar in the *Star*, featuring a new cookie recipe every day. I like simple drop cookies with interesting flavours, like this all-time favourite adapted from a recipe created by McCormick, the spice company, to highlight its sesame seeds. Toasted sesame seeds have an assertive flavour that works beautifully in these sugar cookies.

1. In a dry, medium skillet, toast the sesame seeds over medium heat, shaking the skillet often, until golden, about 5 minutes. Set aside.

2. Preheat the oven to 400°F (200°C). Line 2 baking sheets with parchment paper. In a small bowl, whisk together the flour, cream of tartar, baking soda and salt.

3. In a large bowl, and using an electric mixer on medium speed, beat the butter until light and fluffy, 1 to 2 minutes. Add the sugar and beat until well blended. Beat in the egg and vanilla.

4. With the mixer on low speed, beat in half of the flour mixture and 2 tbsp (30 mL) sesame seeds just until blended. Beat in the remaining flour mixture just until blended. Gather the dough into a ball.

5. Spread out the remaining sesame seeds on a plate. Scoop tablespoonfuls of the dough and roll each into a ball. Roll the balls in the sesame seeds to coat completely. (If the dough is too soft to roll, wrap it in plastic wrap and refrigerate it until firm, about 30 minutes.)

6. Put the balls, 2 inches (5 cm) apart, on the prepared baking sheets. Bake in the centre of the oven until the edges of the cookies are lightly browned, 7 to 9 minutes.

7. Let the cookies cool on the baking sheets for 1 minute, then transfer them to wire racks to cool completely. Store in an airtight container at room temperature for up to 1 week.

# TOASTED SESAME SEED COOKIES

《

MAKES ABOUT 24

½ cup (125 mL) sesame seeds
1 cup plus 6 tbsp (340 mL) all-purpose flour
1 tsp (5 mL) cream of tartar
½ tsp (2 mL) baking soda
Pinch table salt
½ cup (125 mL) unsalted butter, at room temperature
¾ cup (185 mL) granulated sugar
1 large egg
½ tsp (2 mL) pure vanilla extract

## » PERSIAN SAFFRON-RAISIN COOKIES

MAKES ABOUT 24

½ tsp (2 mL) well-crumbled
    saffron threads
2 tsp (10 mL) warm water
1 cup plus 2 tbsp (280 mL) all-
    purpose flour
¾ tsp (4 mL) kosher salt
½ tsp (2 mL) baking powder
¾ cup (185 mL) unsalted butter,
    at room temperature
½ cup (125 mL) granulated
    sugar
¼ cup (60 mL) icing sugar
1 large egg, at room temperature
½ tsp (2 mL) pure vanilla extract
¾ cup (185 mL) raisins
    (preferably Thompson)

I was on a chowhounding expedition in 2004 with my friend Jim Leff, co-founder of Chowhound.com, when he gravitated to bright yellow cookies called shirini kishmishi at a Persian grocery store in North York. I've been addicted to them ever since, finding them at just a few shops around the city. After tinkering with many recipes, this is as close as I can get without using yellow food colouring.

**1.** Preheat the oven to 425°F (220°C). Line 2 baking sheets with parchment paper.

**2.** In a small mortar and using a pestle (or in a small bowl using your fingers or the back of a small spoon), grind the saffron to a powder. Stir in the water and set aside.

**3.** In a medium bowl, whisk together the flour, salt and baking powder.

**4.** In a large bowl, and using an electric mixer on medium-high speed, beat together the butter and granulated and icing sugars for 2 minutes. Add the egg, vanilla and saffron mixture and beat for 2 minutes.

**5.** With the mixer on low speed, gradually beat in the flour mixture in several additions just until blended. Stir in the raisins.

**6.** Scoop heaping tablespoonfuls of the dough, about 2 inches (5 cm) apart, onto the prepared baking sheets. Bake in the centre of the oven until the edges of the cookies are golden and crisp-looking but the centres are still puffy, 6 to 8 minutes.

**7.** Let the cookies cool on the baking sheets for 5 minutes, then transfer them to wire racks to cool completely. Store in an airtight container at room temperature for up to 1 week.

"This is a classic! I've used the recipe for eight years and my copy is covered with little notes I've made about it, so you can see it's a 'keeper.'"

**PATTI SANTUCCI**, BURLINGTON, ONT.

These cookies taste just like classic rolled-out shortbread, but are easier to make. The recipe came from Sigrid McFarland, who used to work in the *Star*'s publisher's office. Since it was the recipe most often requested by readers while home economist Mary McGrath wrote for the *Star*, Mary featured it in *A Shortbread Sampler*, a fundraiser for the *Star*'s Fresh Air and Santa Claus Funds that's still sold at the *Star*'s online store (starstore.ca) and The Cookbook Store (cook-book.com).

**1.** Preheat the oven to 325°F (160°C). Line 2 baking sheets with parchment paper.

**2.** In a large bowl, and using an electric mixer on medium speed, beat together the butter and ½ cup (125 mL) icing sugar until creamy, about 2 minutes. Add the cornstarch and vanilla, and beat until blended.

**3.** With the mixer on low speed, gradually beat in the flour in 3 additions until the dough is light and creamy.

**4.** Drop tablespoonfuls of the dough, about 1 inch (2.5 cm) apart, onto the prepared baking sheets. Bake in the centre of the oven until the cookies are golden around the edges and just baked through, 18 to 22 minutes, watching closely.

**5.** Let the cookies cool on the baking sheets for 10 minutes. Dust them with additional icing sugar, if desired, while they're still warm, then transfer them to wire racks to cool completely. Store in an airtight container at room temperature for up to 1 week.

# WHIPPED SHORTBREAD

READERS' CHOICE

MAKES ABOUT 30

1 cup (250 mL) salted butter, at room temperature
½ cup (125 mL) icing sugar, plus more for dusting, if desired
¼ cup (60 mL) cornstarch
½ tsp (2 mL) pure vanilla extract
1-½ cups (375 mL) all-purpose flour

## » MARY MACLEOD'S BROWN-SUGAR SHORTBREAD

MAKES 16

2-½ cups (625 mL) cake-and-pastry flour

⅔ cup (160 mL) packed dark brown sugar

¾ cup (185 mL) cold, salted butter, cut into small pieces

¼ cup (60 mL) salted butter, melted

1 tbsp (15 mL) granulated sugar

¼ tsp (1 mL) ground cinnamon

Mary Macleod, a Scottish-born home economist, founded Mary Macleod's Shortbread (marymacleod.ca) in 1981. Mary produces her handmade shortbread in small batches, using high-quality ingredients and no preservatives. She shared this recipe, unusual for its use of both cold and melted butter, with the *Star*'s now-retired home economist Mary McGrath, who put the recipe in her fundraiser book, *A Shortbread Sampler*.

**1.** Preheat the oven to 300°F (150°C). Line a baking sheet with parchment paper. Using a sifter or a fine-mesh sieve, sift the flour into a medium bowl and add the brown sugar.

**2.** With a pastry blender, 2 knives or your fingertips, cut or rub the cold butter into the flour mixture until the mixture resembles coarse crumbs. Add the melted butter and work it into the mixture until blended.

**3.** Tip the mixture out onto an unfloured work surface and knead it until a soft dough forms, 2 to 3 minutes. Cut the dough in half. Shape each half into a 7-inch (18 cm) round on the prepared baking sheet.

**4.** Using a sharp knife, cut each round into 8 wedges. Prick all over with a fork then, using the tines of the fork, mark the edges decoratively. Bake in the centre of the oven until golden, about 1 hour. When the shortbread is ready, remove the baking sheet from the oven and recut the wedges.

**5.** In a small bowl, stir together the granulated sugar and cinnamon. Sprinkle the sugar mixture over the warm shortbread and let cool on the baking sheet for 10 minutes. With a metal spatula, carefully transfer the shortbread wedges to wire racks to cool completely. Store in an airtight container at room temperature, with wax paper between the layers, for up to 1 week.

There are three things I love about these cookies: milk chocolate chips, mixing the dough by hand, and the way dotting the tops with extra chocolate chips creates real loveliness. They are from London, Ontario, mom Debbie Bullas-Rubini and her son Kyle Rubini and won second place in a chocolate chip cookie contest I helped judge at the Good Food Festival (goodfoodfestival. com) in 2006. They were my top pick.

# MILK CHOCOLATE CHIP COOKIES

«

MAKES ABOUT 36

1 cup (250 mL) milk chocolate chips
½ cup (125 mL) packed light brown sugar
½ cup (125 mL) granulated sugar
½ cup (125 mL) non-hydrogenated, soft, tub margarine
1 large egg
½ tsp (2 mL) pure vanilla extract
1-¼ cups (310 mL) all-purpose flour
½ tsp (2 mL) baking soda
½ tsp (2 mL) kosher salt

**1.** Preheat the oven to 325°F (160°C). Line 2 baking sheets with parchment paper.

**2.** Set aside ¼ cup (60 mL) chocolate chips. In a large bowl, and using a wooden spoon, beat together the brown and granulated sugars and margarine until creamy. Stir in the egg, vanilla and remaining ¾ cup (185 mL) chocolate chips. Add the flour, baking soda and salt, and stir until well mixed and creamy.

**3.** Drop scant tablespoonfuls of the batter, about 2 inches (5 cm) apart, onto the prepared baking sheets. Dot the tops of the cookies evenly with the reserved chocolate chips.

**4.** Bake in the centre of the oven until the edges are lightly browned, 9 to 11 minutes. Let the cookies cool on the baking sheets for 10 minutes, then transfer them to wire racks to cool completely. Store in an airtight container at room temperature for up to 1 week.

"A keeper, awesome! The icing is optional but good!"

**LAUREL HIGGON,** BOWMANVILLE, ONT.

During a mid-life career change, Lorraine Hawley left her job as a product manager in telecommunications, studied cooking and baking at George Brown College, and started Mabel's Bakery (mabelsbakery.ca). This is one of her decadent offerings.

**1.** For the brownies, preheat the oven to 325°F (160°C). Butter an 8-inch (2 L) square baking pan, then lightly dust the pan with a little flour, knocking out the excess.

**2.** In a medium bowl, sift together ½ cup plus 1 tbsp (140 mL) flour, the cocoa powder and salt.

**3.** Set a stainless steel bowl over a saucepan of gently simmering water, making sure the bowl doesn't touch the water. Add the chocolate squares and the butter to the bowl, and stir until melted. Remove the bowl from the heat.

**4.** In a large bowl, gently whisk together the sugar and eggs just until combined. Using a rubber spatula, stir in the melted chocolate mixture until combined. Gradually fold in the flour mixture, then the chocolate chips. Pour the batter into the prepared pan.

**5.** Bake on the middle rack of the oven until a cake tester inserted in the centre comes out with moist crumbs attached, 40 to 50 minutes. Let cool completely in the pan on a wire rack.

**6.** If making the Chocolate Icing, put the chocolate chips in a small bowl. In a small saucepan, bring the cream to a boil over medium-high heat, then immediately pour it over the chocolate chips. Let stand for 1 minute, then whisk until smooth. Spread the icing evenly over the brownies and let cool to room temperature. Cut the brownies into 16 squares. Store in an airtight container at room temperature for up to 2 days.

# TRIPLE CHOCOLATE BROWNIES «

## READERS' CHOICE

MAKES 16

### Brownies
Softened butter for greasing
All-purpose flour for dusting
½ cup plus 1 tbsp (140 mL) all-purpose flour
2 tbsp (30 mL) unsweetened cocoa powder
½ tsp (2 mL) table salt
7 oz (200 g) semi-sweet chocolate squares, chopped
¾ cup (185 mL) unsalted butter
1-½ cups (375 mL) granulated sugar
3 large eggs, at room temperature
1 cup (250 mL) semi-sweet chocolate chips

### Chocolate Icing (optional)
¾ cup (185 mL) semi-sweet chocolate chips
½ cup (125 mL) whipping cream

## » MIKE HARRIS'S ONE-BOWL CHOCOLATE CAKE

### ®EADER®' CHOICE

MAKES 16 SERVINGS

**Chocolate Cake**

Softened butter for greasing

A little all-purpose flour for dusting

1-¾ cups (435 mL) all-purpose flour

1-½ cups (375 mL) packed light brown sugar

¾ cup (185 mL) vegetable oil

½ cup (125 mL) milk

2 large eggs

¼ cup (60 mL) unsweetened cocoa powder

2 tsp (10 mL) baking powder

2 tsp (10 mL) baking soda

1 tsp (5 mL) pure vanilla extract

½ tsp (2 mL) kosher salt

¾ cup (185 mL) boiling water

Icing sugar for dusting (optional)

**Chocolate Icing (optional)**

4 oz (115 g) semisweet chocolate squares or chips

⅓ cup (80 mL) milk or cream

2 tbsp (30 mL) unsalted butter

1-¼ cups (310 mL) icing sugar

1 tsp (5 mL) pure vanilla extract

---

"This is easy to make from beginning to end, and the outcome is a moist, delicious cake which, when served as an after-dinner dessert to a family of seven adults, disappears within 20 minutes."

**ELIZABETH FERNANDES,** SCARBOROUGH, ONT.

*Star* librarian Peggy Mackenzie single-handedly voted this cake into the book. For such a simple recipe, it has a complicated backstory. Former food editor Marion Kane discovered the cake at a party in 1996 when Progressive Conservative Mike Harris was premier of Ontario. It came from Rochelle Rankin (mother of *Star* reporter Jim Rankin), who got it from Mike Harris in 1971 when Mike and Rochelle were public school teachers in North Bay.

Mike Harris wouldn't discuss the cake at the time, but now confirms that he baked it with grade 7 and 8 boys during an elective cooking class. "The recipe has been around for years," he says. "I can't remember the origins of it, but I think it's about time I shared it with my grandkids."

**1.** For the chocolate cake, preheat the oven to 350°F (180°C). Butter a 10-inch (4 L) Bundt pan, then lightly dust the pan with a little flour, knocking out the excess.

**2.** In a large bowl, combine 1-¾ cups (435 mL) flour, the sugar, oil, milk, eggs, cocoa powder, baking powder, baking soda, vanilla and salt. Beat the mixture with a wooden spoon, a whisk or an electric mixer on high speed until smooth. Add the boiling water and mix well. The batter will be quite runny.

**3.** Pour the batter into the prepared pan. Bake in the centre of the oven until the top is dry and the cake springs back when pressed lightly, 30 to 40 minutes. Let the cake cool in the pan for 10 minutes, then remove it from the pan and let cool completely on a wire rack.

**4.** For the Chocolate Icing, if making, heat the chocolate, milk and butter in a small, heavy saucepan over low heat, stirring often, until the chocolate and butter have melted and the mixture is smooth. Remove the saucepan from the heat. Add the icing sugar and vanilla, and whisk until smooth. Transfer the icing to a measuring cup or pitcher.

**5.** Serve cake as is or dusted with sifted icing sugar or frosted with Chocolate Icing if desired.

# » WILLIS DAVIDSON'S FAMOUS FRUITCAKE

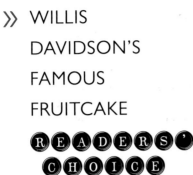

MAKES ABOUT 5 FRUITCAKES
(18 SERVINGS EACH)

**Dried Fruit Mixture**

2-½ cups (625 mL) chopped
   pitted dates
2 cups (500 mL) chopped
   candied citron peel
2 cups (500 mL) seeded raisins
   (Muscat or Lexia)
2 cups (500 mL) Thompson or
   sultana raisins
1-½ cups (375 mL) currants
1-½ cups (375 mL) blanched
   whole almonds
1-½ cups (375 mL) drained
   (reserve syrup) red
   maraschino cherries,
   chopped
½ cup (125 mL) brandy or apple
   juice

**Pineapple Mixture**

1 can (19 oz/540 mL) crushed
   pineapple, undrained
2 cups (500 mL) granulated
   sugar
1 cup (250 mL) strawberry jam
½ cup (125 mL) syrup from the
   maraschino cherries

"Normally, fruitcake is not everyone's favourite but somehow the brandy-soaked cheesecloth method gives the cake an unforgettable flavour. I only make this at Christmas, as mini loaves, and give them away."

**ANTONIETTE VITA,** TORONTO

"Our family has always loved fruitcake and this is a great recipe."

**ROSEMARY ARMSTRONG,** PORT COLBORNE, ONT.

"This is the best fruitcake in the world."

**CARLA MONK,** REABORO, ONT.

"I have used this recipe since 1977 and everyone says it is the best fruitcake they have ever tasted."

**SANDY MARGISON,** TORONTO

This is *Star*'s most requested recipe. It came from a woman named Willis Davidson, a reader from Winchester, Ontario, and my friend Monda Rosenberg discovered it in 1975 when she was a *Star* food writer.

The cake takes two days to make but it's dark and rich, and doesn't have to be aged. The fruit flavour dominates, thanks to strawberry jam and canned pineapple. "I am delighted that my mother's recipe will be included in the new cookbook and I know she would have been very pleased as well," says Lynne Dubbin, the late Willis's daughter.

**1.** On day 1, for the dried fruit mixture, mix together the dates, citron peel, the 2 quantities of raisins, currants, almonds and cherries in a large bowl. Stir in the brandy or apple juice. Cover the bowl with plastic wrap and let stand at room temperature overnight, stirring occasionally.

**2.** For the pineapple mixture, combine the pineapple and sugar in a medium saucepan and bring to a boil over high heat. Reduce the heat to medium-low and simmer, uncovered, stirring often, until the mixture thickens and has reduced to 2-½ cups (625 mL), about 45 minutes.

Remove the saucepan from the heat and stir in the strawberry jam and cherry syrup. Cover and refrigerate overnight.

**3.** On day 2, preheat the oven to 275°F (135°C). Grease five 9- x 5-inch (2 L) loaf pans. Line the pans with parchment paper or aluminum foil, then grease the paper or foil. (You can use other sizes of loaf pans, mini Bundt pans or any pans you like, but adjust the baking time according to whether the pans you use are smaller or larger.)

**4.** For the flour mixture, combine the flour, cinnamon, baking soda, salt, cloves and allspice in a large bowl. Add 1 cup (250 mL) flour mixture to the dried fruit mixture, tossing to thoroughly coat the fruit.

**5.** For the butter mixture, cream the sugar and butter in a very large mixing bowl, using an electric mixer on high speed, until light and fluffy. Beat in the eggs, 1 at a time, beating well after each addition.

**6.** Using a wooden spoon, stir small amounts of the flour and pineapple mixtures into the butter mixture, alternating mixtures, until all is incorporated. Mix well, then stir in the dried fruit mixture.

**7.** Divide the batter among the prepared pans, filling each one about three-quarters full. Put a large, shallow roasting pan half full of hot water on the bottom rack of the oven. Put the loaf pans on the middle rack of the oven and bake until the cakes are darkly golden, a cake tester inserted in the centres comes out with no crumbs attached (if there's fruit, that's okay) and, when pressed, the tops of the cakes are fairly firm, 2-½ to 3-½ hours.

**8.** Let the cakes cool in the pans for 10 minutes, then remove them from the pans, discarding the parchment or foil, and let cool completely on wire racks.

**9.** If you want to age the cakes, cut 5 pieces of cheesecloth, each large enough to wrap 1 cake. Soak the pieces of cheesecloth in brandy or apple juice, then squeeze them out. Wrap each cake in soaked cheesecloth, then plastic wrap, then foil and store in a cool place. (Do not freeze the cakes as this will prevent the flavours from developing.) If desired, occasionally unwrap the foil and plastic wrap and, using a pastry brush, brush the cheesecloth-wrapped cakes with more brandy or apple juice.

**Flour Mixture**

4 cups (1 L) all-purpose flour
2 tsp (10 mL) ground cinnamon
1-½ tsp (7 mL) baking soda
1 tsp (5 mL) table salt
½ tsp (2 mL) ground cloves
½ tsp (2 mL) ground allspice

**Butter Mixture**

2 cups (500 mL) granulated sugar
2 cups (500 mL) unsalted butter, at room temperature
12 large eggs

**For aging (optional)**

Cheesecloth
Brandy or apple juice

# My Favourite Places To Shop

WE'RE FORTUNATE in Greater Toronto to have so many opportunities to try—and buy—foods from many different cultures. Here's a list of my go-to stores for the best and most diverse ingredients:

**Arz Fine Foods** (1909 Lawrence Ave. E., arzbakery.com) is a Middle Eastern fine food shop that's a source of za'atar, bulgur, pomegranate molasses, olives and more. Don't miss the bakery café (and the za'atar croissants) in the back.

**Asian Food Centre** (multiple GTA locations, asianfoodcentre.ca) has everything you need for South Asian cooking, including ready-made dosa batter.

**Bulk Barn** (many locations, bulkbarn.ca) makes buying small amounts of dried spices affordable.

**The Big Carrot** (348 Danforth Ave., thebigcarrot.ca) is a natural food store with ethically sourced meats, bulk dried goods, organics and even Japanese ingredients.

**BJ Supermarket** (1449 Gerrard St. E.) is my go-to shop for Indian ingredients. It's in Gerrard India Bazaar, across from my favourite dosa spot, Udupi Palace.

**The Cookbook Store** (850 Yonge St., cook-book.com) is an independent shop that gives great advice.

**Desta Gebeya Market** (843 Danforth Ave.) is an Ethiopian butcher shop that sells spices like berbere as well as injera (a spongy flatbread).

**Evergreen Brick Works Farmers' Market** (550 Bayview Ave., ebw.evergreen.ca) runs throughout the year on Saturday mornings, featuring farmers and food vendors.

**Farmers' Markets Ontario** (farmersmarketsontario.com) posts a comprehensive market list.

**Fiesta Farms** (200 Christie St., fiestafarms.ca) is an independent, Ontario-minded supermarket that should be cloned.

**Fresh From The Farm** (350 Donlands Ave., freshfromthefarm.ca) is my go-to spot for holiday turkey. It sells hormone-free and drug-free meats, produce and other products from Ontario Amish and Mennonite farmers.

**Friends Fine Food & Groceries** (1881 Yonge St., entrance on Balliol St.) is a small, Persian grocery store. It sells my favourite saffron-raisin cookies.

**Galleria Supermarket** (865 York Mills Rd., galleriasm.com, plus a Thornhill branch at 7171 Yonge St.) is great for Korean groceries, including meat for bulgogi, galbi and pork bone soup. Don't miss the spicy fried chicken (made to order) in the prepared food area/café.

**Hooked** (888 Queen St. E., hookedinc.ca) is a fishmonger

run by chefs Dan and Kristin Donovan who source sustainably caught or responsibly grown, mostly Canadian and American fish and seafood. There's also a teaching kitchen.

**House of Spice** (190 Augusta Ave., Kensington Market, ehouseofspice.com) is a family-run shop with ingredients from around the world (including Ethiopian berbere).

**Iqbal Halal Foods** (2 Thorncliffe Park Dr., iqbalhalalfoods.com) is a large, Pakistani-Indian supermarket.

**J-Town** (Units 6–11, 3160 Steeles Ave. E., Markham, jtown.ca) is a small Japanese shopping mall with a bakery, butcher shop, grocery shop, café and more.

**Loblaws** (many locations) is a block from the *Star* so I shop here much more than at other chains. I appreciate the natural food section and the black label spices like za'atar, harissa and garam masala.

**New Spiceland** (Units 4–6, 5790 Sheppard Ave. E., and 6065 Steeles Ave. E., newspiceland.ca) is a Sri Lankan supermarket.

**Paramount Butcher Shop** (4646 Heritage Hills Blvd., Mississauga, paramountbutchershop.com) is a gourmet halal butcher shop.

**Perola's Supermarket** (247 Augusta Ave., Kensington Market) is my favourite store for Mexican and Latin groceries, including dried chilies, corn tortillas and canned hominy.

**Sanagan's Meat Locker** (176 Baldwin St., Kensington Market, sanagansmeatlocker.com) is a butcher shop run by chef Peter Sanagan, who specializes in meat (and offal) from small Ontario farmers.

**Sanko Trading Co**. (730 Queen St. W., toronto-sanko.com) is a small but well-stocked Japanese shop.

**Segovia Meat Market** (218 Augusta Ave.) has a dazzling array of sausages.

**Spice Trader** (877 Queen St. W., thespicetrader.ca) carries hard-to-find spices like fennel pollen. It offers online sales.

**Sunny Food Mart** (747 Don Mills Rd., sunnysupermarket.com) is a multicultural grocery store with a Chinese bent.

**T&T Supermarket** (222 Cherry St., plus other GTA locations, tnt-supermarket. com,) is everything you could want in an Asian supermarket.

**Taste of Turkiye** (982 Danforth Ave.) is a Turkish/Mediterranean fine food shop. Try the simit, a sesame seed Turkish bagel.

**Trupti Enterprises** (Unit 40, 2 Thorncliffe Park Dr., trupti.ca) is an Indian spice shop that roasts, grinds and mixes most of its offerings.

**Woori Meat Shop** (157 Dundas St. E., Mississauga) is a great Korean butcher shop.

# Thanks

Huge thanks to publisher Robert McCullough, who agreed to lunch at Vij's Rangoli in Vancouver to listen to my book pitches, and championed this project for his fabulous new imprint Appetite by Random House.

Monda Rosenberg, Cynthia David, Alison Maclean, Kirsten Hanson, Dana McCauley, Alison Fryer, Cinda Chavich and Julian Armstrong guided me down the cookbook path by sharing connections and advice about the mysterious world of publishing.

At the *Toronto Star*, my gratitude goes to Phil Bingley for hiring me, Lesley Taylor for giving me my dream job in food, and Mo Gannon, Kim Honey and Janet Hurley for letting me keep it. Thanks to Eddie Greenspon and Robin Graham for letting this book happen, Dan Smith for listening, and Lynne Munro for her promotion expertise and passion for this project.

Big thanks to former Saucy Lady Amy Pataki, Food Dude Jon Filson and Fare Lady Susan Sampson for sharing food duties with me over the years. It's lonely working alone now.

Eric Vellend gets a special shout-out. As a freelancer, he handled our weekly Chef's Showcase recipe in the *Star*'s TV guide for two years and brought in many of the chef recipes in this book.

Freelance writers Habeeb Salloum, Cynthia David, Smita Chandra, Corey Mintz and Linda Barnard also contributed important recipes. So did my mother-in-law Margaret MacKenzie.

My Chicago literary agent, Amy Collins, and Toronto lawyer and friend, Kate Henderson, helped negotiate my 10-page contract. Random House's director of contracts, Samantha North, was so patient that I thoroughly enjoyed the process.

My husband, Rick MacKenzie, happily did almost all of my grocery shopping (including more than 100 trips in two months). My teenager, Lucy, watched six seasons of *Criminal Minds* with me to relax at night. My enthusiastic four-year-old, Hazel, said, "Put it in the cookbook" to everything I "made" (including sliced cucumbers).

I couldn't have written this book without my sister-in-law Jennifer Wells and brother Michael Bain, who took Hazel to play with her cousins Kate, Gillian and Archie on multiple weekends after Rick returned to our ranch in Alberta for spring planting.

Thanks to everyone who ate my food, helped me de-stress and/or just listened, especially Kim Honey, Amy Pataki, the Mahjong Girls (Maureen Mahan, Sandra Edmunds and Leslie Edmunds), Cynthia Lewis, Amy Bodman, Jennifer Goad, Franci Duran, Gillian Talacko, Adrienne Amato, Jo-Ann Dodds, Kate Robertson, Erika Tustin, Peggy Mackenzie, Astrid Lange, Kathleen Power and all the hungry souls in the *Toronto Star* Life section and library. Megan Ogilvie gave me lots of great advice while writing her own book.

The *Star*'s Christine Loureiro steered me to photographer Ryan Szulc and prop stylist Madeleine Johari who, along with food stylist Noah Witenoff and photography assistant Matthew Gibson, were a dream team. The six-day photo shoot for this book was creative and calm, and the results still take my breath away.

Thanks to all the unsung heroes at Random House of Canada who turned a manuscript into a book, starting with Lindsay Paterson, assistant to the publisher. We swapped many an email between Vancouver and Toronto. In Toronto, managing editor Susan Burns and designer Terri Nimmo were good-humoured, gracious and patient through multiple rounds of layout and cover design. Julia Aitken was a laser-sharp copy editor. Lesley Cameron took on the proofreading and Lana Okerlund put together the index. Thanks in advance to publicity manager Josh Glover, director of strategic marketing Cathy Paine, and director of special sales Marlene Fraser who'll be heavily involved in promoting and selling this cookbook.

Biggest and final thanks to my mom, Barbara, for teaching me to cook, and my dad, Harry, for teaching me to fish.

# Index

Note: Page numbers in italics refer to photographs.